The Symbolic Execution of Software

COMPUTER SCIENCE: RESEARCH AND PRACTICE

Series Editors: *Alan Brown, Software Engineering Institute, Carnegie Mellon University, Pittsburgh, USA*
Norman Fenton, Centre for Software Reliability, City University, London, UK

The aim of this series is to provide a route for rapid publication of up-to-date industrial and academic research material in Computer Science, hence, academic studies, industrial techniques, and collaborative academic/industrial research work are all of potential interest to this series. A typical subject for a book in the series may be an analysis of a research topic, the results from analytical experiments, a discussion of an innovative industrial technique or material from an advanced tutorial or taught course. As a result, books in the series may take a number of forms - edited volumes, a write-up of a research project, a technical monograph or an advanced text book - but in all cases work will be placed in context to be of interest to as wide a computer science community as possible.

Titles in this series

1. *Logic and Specification*
   Extending VDM-SL *for advanced formal specification*
   C. Middleburg

2. *The Symbolic Execution of Software*
   The SYM-BOL system
   D. Coward and D. Ince

3. *Software Quality Assurance and Measurement*
   A worldwide perspective
   Edited by N. Fenton, R. Whitty and Y. Iizuka

4. *Software Measurement*
   Understanding software engineering
   Edited by A. Melton

The Symbolic Execution of Software

The SYM-BOL system

David Coward

Principal Lecturer in Computing,
University of the West of England,
Bristol, UK

and

Darrel Ince

Professor of Computing,
The Open University,
Milton Keynes, UK

CHAPMAN & HALL

London · Glasgow · Weinheim · New York · Tokyo · Melbourne · Madras

Published by Chapman & Hall, 2-6 Boundary Row, London SE1 8HN

Chapman & Hall, 2-6 Boundary Row, London SE1 8HN, UK

Blackie Academic & Professional, Wester Cleddens Road, Bishopbriggs, Glasgow G64 2NZ, UK

Chapman & Hall GmbH, Pappelallee 3, 69469 Weinheim, Germany

Chapman & Hall USA, One Penn Plaza, 41st Floor, New York NY 10119, USA

Chapman & Hall Japan, ITP-Japan, Kyowa Building, 3F, 2-2-1 Hirakawacho, Chiyoda-ku, Tokyo 102, Japan

Chapman & Hall Australia, Thomas Nelson Australia, 102 Dodds Street, South Melbourne, Victoria 3205, Australia

Chapman & Hall India, R. Seshadri, 32 Second Main Road, CIT East, Madras 600 035, India

First edition 1995

© 1995 David Coward and Darrel Ince

Printed in Great Britain by Clays Ltd, St Ives plc

ISBN   0 412 58340 2

A catalogue record for this book is available from the British Library

∞ Printed on permanent acid-free text paper, manufactured in accordance with ANSI/NISO Z39.48-1992 and ANSI/NISO Z39.48-1984 (Permanence of Paper).

Contents

1 Testing   **1**
   1.1 Introduction   1
   1.2 Software product testing   3
   1.3 What this book is about   4

2 Tools and techniques for testing   **7**
   2.1 Functional versus structural testing   7
   2.2 Effectiveness of program testing techniques   22
   2.3 The evaluation of testing techniques   28
   2.4 Summary   29

3 The principles of symbolic execution   **31**
   3.1 Introduction   31
   3.2 Symbolic evaluation   31
   3.3 An example of simple symbolic execution   33
   3.4 Simplification of symbolic expressions   46
   3.5 Problems in applying symbolic execution   46
   3.6 Applications of symbolic execution   52

4 Existing symbolic execution systems   **61**
   4.1 Minimum features of a symbolic execution testing system   61
   4.2 Strengths and weaknesses of current systems   64
   4.3 The ideal symbolic execution testing system   71
   4.4 Ideal, existing and new symbolic execution systems   73
   4.5 Weaknesses of symbolic execution   78
   4.6 The remainder of this book   81

5 SYM-BOL – a symbolic execution system for COBOL   **83**
   5.1 Environment   83
   5.2 Input   83
   5.3 Output   83
   5.4 User strategies   85
   5.5 The remainder of this book   89

6 **The main features of SYM-BOL**   **91**
  6.1 Assertions   91
  6.2 Transforming a source program into intermediate form   100
  6.3 Path selection and symbolic execution   110
  6.4 Determining path feasibility and test generation   115

7 **Conclusions**   **129**
  7.1 Introduction   129
  7.2 Problems of applying symbolic execution   129
  7.3 Practicality of a COBOL symbolic execution testing system   131
  7.4 Strengths of the SYM-BOL system   132
  7.5 Weaknesses of the SYM-BOL system   132
  7.6 Symbolic execution and the general features of programming
       languages   133
  7.7 Concluding remarks   140
  7.8 Conclusion   142

Appendix A   **143**

References   **147**

Index   **152**

CHAPTER 1

Testing

1.1 Introduction

This book is concerned with program testing and in particular with symbolic execution as a technique for aiding program testing. The term 'testing' is often used to describe techniques of checking software by means of execution with test data. However, a wider meaning will be assumed in this work. We shall assume that testing includes any technique which involves the checking of software; for example – program proving – as well as conventional testing: the execution of test cases. The word 'checking' implies that a comparison is undertaken; this is often made between the output from a test and an expected output derived by the tester. The expected output is usually based on some specification from which the tester derives the expected result – usually by hand.

Two terms often associated with testing are verification and validation. **Verification** refers to those checking activities which ensure correctness from one phase to another phase of the software development cycle. A good example of this is module testing, where a module is tested against its functional specification. **Validation** involves checking the software against some requirements specification. A good example of this activity is system testing. Sometimes, usually in American texts, verification is associated with formal proofs of correctness, while validation is used to describe the execution of a system or part of a system with test data. This book avoids these terms and instead refers only to testing. This book will also refer to both functional and non-functional requirements. The former are requirements which express some action that a system should carry out, for example, the fact that it should produce a series of reports. The latter are constraints on a system which usually provide some envelope governing performance. Typical non-functional requirements include those concerned with response time, memory occupancy and reliability.

Program testing is one of many activities that comprise the larger, complex task of software development. We can regard the development of a software product as a series of transformations from one level of abstraction to the next, culminating in the delivery of an executable system. The need for program testing arises out of an inability to guarantee that the earlier activities such as system design have been performed adequately.

Testing is an activity which attempts to assess how well earlier transformations have been performed.

Software development starts when a customer identifies some need. This need is expressed in terms of functions and constraints. An example of the latter is the constraint that a system must fit into some maximum amount of memory. Producing software which provides the required functions does not imply that all the requirements have been satisfied. Additional requirements may be that the system satisfies legal obligations, that it performs within specified response times that it meets documentation standards, or that it is developed according to some particular house style to enable easier modification. This book addresses the testing of functional requirements and does not concern itself with testing constraints.

Functional testing may be employed when testing a new system or when testing a system that has been modified during maintenance. **Regression testing** is the name given to functional testing which follows modification. Primarily, regression testing is undertaken to determine whether a correction has altered the functions of the software that were intended to remain unchanged.

It is easy to define levels of abstraction through which software development passes. One such series is:

- requirements analysis;
- requirements specification;
- software design;
- programming.

Each of the transformations between levels of abstraction may introduce additional faults. A programmed system which contains faults will not be congruent with the software design; the software design may, in turn, contain faults preventing it matching the requirements specification, and so on. Even the first level of abstraction, the requirements specification, may contain faults in that it does not reflect the real requirements of a customer.

To help overcome this tendency for increasing fault incidence with increasing levels of abstraction, testing should take place at each level: module testing, integration testing, system testing and acceptance testing. Discovery of faults at a particular level of abstraction may cause development to return to a previous level or several earlier levels of abstraction before the source of the problem is discovered.

Testing at each level of abstraction is not easy. The software can be tested by executing it with test cases. This is not generally possible for the higher levels of abstraction such as requirements definition where alternative techniques are necessary. There are some exceptions to this where specifications written in notations such as VDM can be executed, albeit inefficiently, and hence tested in much the same way as the software itself [Hek85]. It is worth noting at this point that although advances in formal specification have brought greater confidence in the correctness of specifications and designs, most software developers still use execution of the software as the final demonstration of correctness.

1.2 Software product testing

A software product consists of several components: the executable software, software documentation, user documentation, etc. All of these components should be fit for purpose before release and so each requires checking. This book is concerned with testing only the software component.

The literature is not united about the aims of software testing. Testing encompasses the detection of errors during development and also the process of checking the requirements. The goals of testing by execution are unclear. On the one hand testing is concerned with finding faults in the software: on the other, it is concerned with demonstrating that there are no faults in the software, though it is difficult to see how this may be fully done other than by formal verification.

These differing perspectives can be viewed as an individual's attitude towards testing which may have an impact on how testing is conducted. Aiming to find faults is a destructive process, whereas aiming to demonstrate that there are no faults is constructive. Adopting the latter strategy may cause the tester to be less stringent in testing, giving rise to the risk of missing faults. The destructive stance is perhaps more likely to uncover faults because it is more probing. Weinberg [Wei73] suggests that programmers regard the software they produce as an extension of their ego. To be destructive in testing is therefore difficult. NASA appears to have believed this for many years having, in 1975, established teams of software validators separated from the software creators [Spe84].

An alternative view is that testing passes through two distinct phases. Few people with any experience of writing programs would begin testing by expecting the program to be correct, i.e. without any faults. Therefore the first phase of testing is where errors are expected to be detected. Once these errors have been found the cause must be found. The location of faults – debugging – is an associated but distinct activity. On locating a fault it must be corrected and testing continued.

Gradually, as the detection of errors becomes less frequent, the role of testing changes. A second phase of testing commences in which the aim is to demonstrate that the program is now correct, i.e. free from faults.

Precisely when the transition from the first phase of testing to the second phase takes place is not easy to define. When the tester begins to feel confident that the faults have been removed seems intuitively correct, but we do not have a measure of this confidence. Similarly, it is difficult to state the circumstances when the test reverts to phase one after a fault is discovered in phase two.

There are many questions concerning testing which are difficult to answer:

- How much testing should be undertaken?
- When should we have confidence in the software?
- When a fault is discovered, should we be pleased that it has been found, or dismayed that it existed?
- Does the discovery of a fault lead us to suspect that there are likely to be more faults and, the more faults we find, the more we suspect are left waiting to be discovered?
- At what stage can we feel confident that all, or realistically most, of the faults have been discovered?
- To what extent is testing concerned with quality assurance?
- What is the relationship between testing and the creation of fault tolerant software?

Testing is about both finding faults and demonstrating their absence. This is achieved by setting out to find faults. These views are reconciled by establishing the notion of the 'thoroughness of testing'. Where testing has been thorough, faults found and corrected, re-tested with equal thoroughness, then we have established confidence in the software. If, on the other hand, we have no feel for the thoroughness of the test we have no means of establishing confidence in the results of the testing. Much work has been done to establish test metrics to assess the thoroughness of a set of tests and to develop techniques that facilitate thorough testing. These are discussed in Chapter 2.

1.3 What this book is about

Chapter 2 examines the various tools and techniques of testing that have been researched. It examines some of the really tough questions that testing researchers set out to solve such as: when do we stop testing?

Chapter 3 describes symbolic execution in a great deal of detail. It examines how symbolic execution is carried out, and the major questions that have been posed by researchers in this area. It also provides a basic vocabulary which will enable the reader to access the remainder of this book.

One of the big advantages of symbolic execution is that it can be used in a variety of ways in a software project. For example, it can be used as a front-end to the process of deriving structural test data automatically. Chapter 3 concludes by examining the main applications of the technique.

Symbolic execution requires extensive tool support. Chapter 4 looks at existing symbolic execution systems. It specifies the minimum facilities expected in such systems and critically evaluates existing systems with respect to the facilities.

Chapter 4 concludes by summarising the weaknesses of symbolic execution as a testing technique and the weaknesses of the tools that have been constructed to support its application. Second, it establishes a set of research aims whose solution is described in the following two chapters.

Chapter 5 outlines the main facilities of a symbolic execution system called SYM-BOL which executes COBOL programmes.

Chapter 6 describes SYM-BOL in more detail and shows how SYM-BOL can be seen as an attempt to overcome many of the weaknesses summarised in Chapter 4.

Chapter 7 is a summary chapter and outlines some of the areas in symbolic execution where further work is needed.

CHAPTER 2

Tools and techniques for testing

There are many widely differing testing techniques. But, for all the apparent diversity, they cluster according to their underlying principles. There are two major dimensions to testing strategy: the functional/structural dimension and the static/dynamic dimension. A purely functional strategy uses only the requirements, defined in the requirements specification, as the basis for testing; whereas a structural strategy is based on the detailed design or implemented source code and uses structural information such as paths. A dynamic approach executes the software and assesses the performance, while a static approach analyses the software without recourse to its execution.

2.1 Functional versus structural testing

A testing strategy may start by considering the requirements specification or by examining the software. When starting from the requirements specification the required functions are identified; then the software is tested to assess whether the functions are implemented correctly. This is known as **functional testing**.

In starting from the software the structure is identified and used to derive test cases which, in turn, are used to assess whether the software meets a specification. This is known as **structural testing**. When developing a new program based on an existing program, where only a subset of the functions are required, it is all to easy to accidentally incorporate unnecessary functions; these functions which are included in the software, but not required, are more likely to be identified by adopting a structural testing strategy in preference to a functional testing strategy. The converse will normally be true for errors of omission.

2.1.1 Functional testing

Functional testing involves two steps. First, identify the functions which the software is expected to perform. Second, create test data which will check whether these functions are implemented in the software. No consideration is given to how the program performs these functions. This approach is used during system and acceptance testing, although a form of technical functional testing occurs during the testing of modules.

There have been significant moves towards the more systematic creation of requirement specifications and design [Dem81, Hay87, Jac75, Jon86]. This may be expected to lead to a more systematic approach to functional testing. For example, rules can be constructed for the direct identification of functions and data from systematic design documentation. Unfortunately, these rules do not take account of likely fault classes. Weyuker and Ostrand [Wey80] have suggested that the next step in the development of functional testing is a method of formal design documentation which includes a description of faults associated with each part of the design as well as the design features themselves.

Howden [How81] has also posited that this method be taken further. It is not sufficient to identify classes of faults for parts of the design. Isolation of particular properties of each function should take place. Each property will have certain fault classes associated with it.

There are many classifications of faults. A detailed classification is given by Chan [Cha79] which is a refinement of Van Tassel's classification [Van78]. Chan's classification consists of 13 groups which are sub-divided to produce a total of 47 categories. Kaner [Kan93] has also identified 13 major categories which give a total of over 400 specific errors.

Functional testing has been termed a **black box** approach as it treats the program as a box with its contents hidden from view. Testers submit test cases to the program based on their understanding of the intended function of the program.

A term often used in conjunction with functional testing is **oracle**. This is someone who can state precisely what the outcome of a program will be for a particular case. Such an oracle does not always exist and, at best, it may only be an imprecise expectations [Wey82]. Simulation software provides a powerful illustration of this problem. No precise expectation can be determined and the most precise expectation that can be provided is a range of plausible values.

2.1.2 Structural testing

The opposite strategy to the black box approach is the white box approach. Here, testing is based upon the detailed design or source code rather than on the functions required of the program – hence the term structural testing. This approach is usually used during module testing and integration testing.

While functional testing necessitates the execution of the program there are two strategies for structural testing. The first strategy – and the one most commonly practised – is to execute the program with test cases. Second, and less common, the functions of the program are compared with the required functions for congruence. The second of these approaches is characterized to some extent by symbolic execution and more accurately by program proving.

Structural testing that involves execution of the program may require the execution of a single path through the program, or that a particular level of use has been made of all the code. The notion of a minimally-thorough test has occupied research efforts over the years. Some examples of what constitutes a minimally-thorough test of a program are shown below:

- All statements in the programs should be executed at least once [Mil63].

- All branches in the program should be executed at least once [Mil63].

- All linear code sequence and jumps (LCSAJ) in the program should be executed at least once [Woo 80]. An LCSAJ is a sequence of code ending with a transfer of control out of the linear code sequence.

Achieving each of these is necessary for a good test to be performed on a program. To achieve a given level of coverage requires that all earlier level metrics have been attained. The best test is an exhaustive test where all paths through the program are domain tested. There are two obstacles to this goal which account for the existence of the other measures listed above.

The first obstacle is the large number of possible paths. The number of paths is determined by the number of conditions and loops in the program. All combinations of the conditions must be considered and cause a rapidly increasing number of combinations as the number of conditions increases. Loops add to the combinatorial explosion: they give rise to an excessively large number of paths. This is most acute when the number of iterations is not fixed but is determined by input variables.

The second obstacle is the number of infeasible paths. An infeasible path is one which cannot be executed due to contradiction occurring at some of the predicates associated conditional statements. It is surprising that, in a sample of programs, of the 1000 shortest paths only 18 were feasible [Hed81].

In order to illustrate path coverage consider the program fragment shown below*:

```
1   accept a
2   if a > 15
3   then
4      compute b = b + 1
5   else
6      compute c = c + 1
7   end-if
8   if a < 10
9   then
```

---

* This program is expressed in the dialect of COBOL used in later stages of this book. An appendix summarises the main features of the language.

10   compute $d = d + 1$
11 **end-if**

There are four paths through, they are:

Path 1   1,2,3,4,7,8,11.
Path 2   1,2,5,6,7,8,9,10,11.
Path 3   1,2,5,6,7,8,11.
Path 4   1,2,3,4,7,8,9,10,11.

Path 1 can be executed so long as the value of a is greater than 15 after the execution of line 1. Path 2 can be executed so long as the value of a is less than 10 after the execution of line 1. Path 3 can be executed so long as the value of a lies in the range 10 to 15 inclusive after the execution of line 1. Path 4 cannot be executed regardless of the value of a because a cannot be both greater than 15 and less than 10 simultaneously. Hence this path is infeasible.

Even trivial programs contain a large number of paths. Where a program contains a loop which may be executed a variable number of times the number of paths increases dramatically. A path exists for each of the following circumstances:

- where the loop is not executed;
- where the loop is executed once;
- where the loop is executed twice... etc.

The number of paths is dependent on the value of the variable controlling the loop. This poses a problem for those who adopt a structural testing strategy: how many of the variable-controlled, loop-derived paths should be covered? Miller and Paige [Mil74] sought to tackle this problem by introducing the notion of a level-i path.

A level-0 path leads from an entrance to the software to an output, without executing any branch more than once. Any loop that exists on the level-0 path is executed only once when it is executed. A level-1 path is a series of consecutive branches that have already been included on a level-0 path. Thus a level-1 path is part of a level-0 path that is to be repeated just once. Similarly, a level-2 path is part of a level-1 path that is to be executed once more than on the level-1 path, i.e. three times.

A possible structural testing strategy might be to attempt to execute the greatest level path **lgp**. By attempting to execute **lgp** first, many of the branches on lesser level paths (ancestral paths) will be collaterally executed. In other words, when executing the deepest level-i path many other ancestral paths will necessarily be executed as part of that execution. This reduces the number of tests required to execute the remaining unexecuted branches.

Because the testing of every path is generally impossible, branch coverage is commonly used as a metric. However, achieving a high branch coverage is not a simple matter, the main hindrance to this being infeasible paths. The difficulty becomes apparent when a feasible path is sought for a particular branch. Many of the selected paths may be found to be infeasible and pinpointing a feasible path can require a large amount of effort devoted to searching for it.

A further difficulty in achieving complete coverage of a testing metric is the presence of island code. This is a sequence of lines of code following a transfer of control or program termination which is not the destination of a transfer of control from elsewhere in the program. An example of island code is a procedure that is not invoked. Island code should not exist; it is normally caused by an error in the invocation of a required procedure, or the failure to recognize redundant code following a maintenance change.

2.1.3 Static versus dynamic analysis

A testing technique that does not involve the execution of the software with data is known as **static analysis**. This includes program proving, symbolic execution and anomaly analysis. Program proving involves rigorously specifying constraints on the input and output data sets for a software component such as a procedure. The proof is created by demonstrating that each sequence of steps in the procedure causes the input to be transformed to the output. Symbolic execution—which is the subject of this book—creates expressions for the output variables on a path in terms of input variables and constants. Anomaly analysis searches the program source for anomalous features such as island code.

Dynamic analysis requires that the software be executed. The goal is to achieve a certain level of program test effectiveness where, for example, a coverage metric such as the proportion of coverage of branches in a program may be used to assess the effectiveness of a test. Test data is created and, following execution, the output is compared with the expectation. Following a test execution the values for the program test effectiveness metrics are reported. Dynamic analysis can be regarded as a form of automatic documentation of the execution of software.

The recording of test effectiveness metrics during dynamic analysis relies on the use of probes inserted into the program [Pai74]. These probe statements make calls to analysis routines which record the frequency of execution. As a result the extent of statement, branch, LCSAJ or any other coverage metric can be reported on completion of execution. The code not exercised by the testing is normally listed as well.

Dynamic analysis can be used in conjunction with assertions. These are statements about the values of variables which can be incorporated at particular points in the program. Should these assertions be violated during execution the dynamic analysis would report the details of the violation.

Dynamic analysis can act as a bridge between functional and structural

Table 2.1 *A taxonomy of testing methods.*

	Structural	*Functional*
Static	Symbolic execution	
	Partition analysis	
	Program proving	
	Anomaly analysis	
Dynamic	Computation testing	Random testing
	Domain testing	Equivalence partitioning
	Path-based testing	Decision tables
	Mutation analysis	Adaptive testing

testing. Initially functional testing may dictate the set of test cases. The execution of these test cases may be monitored by dynamic analysis. The program can then be examined structurally to determine test cases which will exercise the code left idle by the previous test. This dual approach results in the program being tested for the functions required and the whole of the program being exercised. The latter ensures that the program does not perform any function that is not required.

2.1.4 A taxonomy of testing techniques

Over the last 15 years many testing techniques have been established. There is no generally accepted testing technique taxonomy. The degree to which the techniques employ a static v dynamic analysis strategy or a functional v structural strategy varies and provides the basis for a simple classification of testing techniques. The grid in Table 2.1 outlines one classification. The techniques are described later in the chapter.

Static-structural

Here no execution of the software is undertaken. Assessment is made of the soundness of the software by criteria other than its run-time behaviour. The features assessed vary with the technique. For example, anomaly analysis checks for peculiar features such as the existence of island code; on the other hand, program proving aims to demonstrate congruence between the specification and the software.

The first static-structural technique is **symbolic execution**, sometimes referred to as symbolic evaluation. This does not execute a program in the traditional sense. The traditional notion of execution requires that a selection of paths through the program is exercised by a set of cases. In symbolic execution the cases consisting of actual data values are replaced by symbolic values. A program normally executed using inputs consisting of actual data values results in the output of a series of actual values. Sym-

		Path condition	A	B	C	D
1	accept a		a			
2	accept b		a	b		
3	accept c		a	b	c	
4	accept d		a	b	c	d
5	compute $a = a + b$		$a+b$	b	c	d
6	if $a > c$	$a + b \leq c$	$a+b$	b	c	d
7	then $d = d + 1$					
8	endif	$a + b \leq c$	$a+b$	b	c	d
9	if $b = d$	$a + b \leq c$	$a+b$	b	c	d
10	then print 'success' a, d					
11	else print 'fail' a, d	$a + b \leq c \wedge b \neq d$	$a+b$	b	c	d
12	endif	$a + b \leq c \wedge b \neq d$	$a+b$	b	c	d

Figure 2.1 *Symbolic path execution.*

bolic execution, on the other hand, produces a set of algebraic expressions, one expression per output variable. It occupies a middle ground of testing between executing with test data and program proving.

There are a number of symbolic execution systems [Boy75, Cla76b, Kin76, Ram76]. The most common approach to symbolic execution is to perform an analysis of the program resulting in the creation of a flowgraph. This is a directed graph which contains decision points and assignments associated with each branch. By traversing the flowgraph from an entry point, through a particular path, a list of assignment statements and branch predicates is produced. The execution part of the approach takes place by following the path from top to bottom. During this path traversal each input variable is given a symbol in place of an actual value. Thereafter, each assignment statement is evaluated so that it is expressed in terms of symbolic values of input variables and constants.

Consider path 1, 2, 3, 4, 5, 6, 8, 9, 11, 12 through the program fragment shown as Figure 2.1. The symbolic values of the variables and the path condition at each branch are given in the right-hand columns for the evaluation of this path. At the end of the symbolic execution of a path the output variables will be represented by expressions in terms of input variables and constants expressed as symbolic expressions. The output expressions will be subject to constraints. A list of these constraints is provided by the set of symbolic representations of each condition predicate along the path. Analysis of these constraints may indicate that the path is not executable due to a contradiction. This problem is encountered in all forms of path testing.

The output expressions from symbolic execution are examined to ensure that they do not conflict with the assertions. In the example shown in Figure 2.1 only the symbolic expressions for *a* and *d* will be of interest as these are the only output variables.

A major difficulty with symbolic execution is the handling of loops. Should loops be symbolically evaluated once, twice, a hundred times or not at all? Some symbolic executors take a pragmatic approach. For each loop three paths are constructed, each path containing one of the following: no execution of the loop, a single execution of the loop and two executions of the loop. Symbolic execution does not specify the number of paths that should be considered, nor is there a set of criteria for selecting paths to execute symbolically, but coverage metrics may be used to assess thoroughness.

Partition analysis uses symbolic execution to identify sub-domains of the input data domain. Symbolic execution is performed on both the software and the specification. The path conditions are then used to produce the sub-domains such that each sub-domain is treated identically by both the program and the specification. Where a part of the input domain cannot be allocated to such a sub-domain, then either a structural or functional fault has been discovered. In the partition analysis system described by Richardson and Clarke [Ric81] the specification is expressed in a manner close to program code. This is impractical: specifications need to be written at a higher level of abstraction if this technique is to prove useful.

Program proving is the use of mathematical specifications and proof in order to verify the correctness of a piece of software. The most widely reported approach to program proving is the 'inductive assertion verification' method due to Floyd [Flo67]. In this method assertions are placed at the beginning and end of selected procedures.

> A procedure is said to be correct (with respect to its input and output assertions) if the truth of its input assertion upon procedure entry ensures the truth of its output assertion upon procedure exit [Han76].

There are many similarities between program proving and symbolic execution. Neither technique executes with actual data and both examine the source code. However, program proving aims to be more rigorous in its approach. The main distinction between program proving and symbolic execution is in the area of loop handling. Program proving adopts a theoretical approach. This is in contrast to symbolic execution where an attempt is made to produce a proof that accounts for all possible iterations of the loop. The best that symbolic execution can do is evidenced by some symbolic execution systems that make the assumption that if the loop is correct when not executed, when executed just once and when executed twice, then it will be correct for any number of iterations.

Analysis of the source code is performed in the same manner as for symbolic execution, but the goal is not just a single expression for an output variable. Instead, many points along a path are selected and assertions concerning the state of variables at these points are made. The source code analysis produces expressions at the selected points and a comparison is made between the derived expressions and the assertions. One of the selected points is usually chosen to be a point of output for the path, and at this point the goal of program proving is the same as for symbolic execution: the output of expressions representing variables.

Program proving can be summarized by the following steps:

- Construct a program.
- Examine the program and place assertions at the beginning and end of all procedures blocks.
- Determine whether the code between each pair of start and end assertions will always achieve the end assertion, given the start assertion.
- If the code achieves the end assertions then the block has been proved correct. If the code fails to achieve the end assertion then mistakes have been made in either the program or the proof. The proof and the program should then be checked to determine which of these possibilities has occurred and appropriate corrections made.

DeMillo *et al.* [Dem79] describe how theorems and proofs can never be conceived as 'correct' but rather, only 'acceptable' to a given community. This acceptability is achieved by their being examined by a wide audience who can find no fault in the proof. Confidence in the proof increases as the number of researchers, finding no faults, increases [Lak76]. This approach has clear parallels with the confidence placed in software. The wider the audience that has used the software, and found no fault, the more confidence is invested in the software.

When a program has been proved correct, in the sense that it has been demonstrated that the end assertions will be achieved given the initial assertions, then the program has achieved partial correctness. To achieve total correctness it must also be shown that the program will terminate – in other words that all loops will terminate [Elp72].

The validity of program proving relies upon the notion that it is unlikely that a mistake will be made in a program and a corresponding compensating mistake in the assertions which are the basis of the proof. This is rather optimistic for all but the smallest programs.

Anomaly analysis is a form of static testing. The first level of anomaly analysis is performed by a compiler to determine whether the program adheres to the language syntax. This first level of analysis is not usually considered testing. Testing is usually deemed to commence when a syntactically correct program is produced.

The second level of anomaly analysis searches for anomalies that are not outlawed by the programming language. Examples of such systems which carry out this form of analysis are DAVE [Ost76], FACES [Ram74] and

TOOLPACK [Ost83]. Other systems such as SPADE [Car86] and MALPAS [Web87] also include anomaly analysis as a pre-requisite to other system features. Anomalies which can be discovered by these systems include:

- the existence of unexecutable code (island code);
- problems concerning array bounds;
- failure to initialize variables;
- labels and variables which are unused;
- jumps into and out of loops;
- high complexity;
- departure from programming standards.

Discovery of these classes of problem is dependent on the analysis of the code. The first phase of anomaly analysis is to produce a flowgraph. This representation of the software can then be scanned to identify anomalies.

Some features of anomaly analysis are known as **data flow analysis**. Here emphasis is placed on a careful analysis of the flow of data. Software may be viewed as a flow of data from input to output. Input values contribute to intermediate values which, in turn, determine the output values. Data flow anomalies detected are:

- Assigning values to a variable which is not used later in the program;
- Using a variable (in an expression or condition) which has not previously been assigned a value;
- (Re)assigning a variable without making use of a previously assigned value.

Data flow anomalies may arise from mistakes such as misspelling, confusion of variable names and incorrect parameter passing – a reason why many early systems for detecting anomalies were FORTRAN based. The existence of a data flow anomaly is not evidence of a fault: it merely indicates the possibility of a fault. Software that contains data flow anomalies may be less likely to satisfy the functional requirements than software which does not contain them.

The role of data flow analysis is one of a program critic drawing attention to potentially erroneous uses of variables. These uses must be checked against the programmer's intentions and, if in disagreement, the program should be corrected.

2.1.5 Dynamic-functional

This class of technique executes test cases. No consideration is given to the detailed design of the software. The use of techniques such as decision tables and cause-effect graphing creates test cases from the rules contained in the specification. Alternatively, test cases may be generated randomly. Equivalence partitioning [Mye79] creates test cases based on a decomposition of the required functions. Adaptive perturbation testing [Coo76] attempts to create additional, more effective, test cases by modifying previous test cases. In all these approaches there is the need for an oracle to pronounce on the correctness of the output.

One of the most practical techniques which comes under the dynamic-functional heading is **equivalence partitioning**. The aim of this technique is to devise test cases such that each represents a set of equivalent tests. The set of test cases form an equivalence class. The assumption is that if one test case in the equivalence class detects an error, then all other test cases in the same class will also detect the same error. Equivalence partitioning is the technique of identifying the finite number of equivalence classes and devising a single case to represent the class.

There are two types of equivalence class: valid and invalid. **Valid equivalence classes** are those that the software is required to process. **Invalid equivalence classes** are those that should be rejected. It is important to devise test cases for both types of equivalence class.

Goodenough and Gerhart [Goo75] suggest that

a basic hypothesis for the reliability and validity of testing is that the input domain of a program can be partitioned into a finite number of equivalence classes such that a test of a representative of each class will, by induction, test the entire class, and hence, the equivalent of exhaustive testing of the input domain can be performed.

Random testing produces test data without reference to the code or the specification. The main software tool required is a random number generator. Duran and Ntafos [Dur 81, Dur 84] describe how estimates of the operational reliability of the software can be derived from the results of random testing.

Potentially, there are some problems for random testing. The most significant is that there is no guarantee of complete coverage of the program. For example, when a constraint on a path is an equality e.g. $a = b + 5$ the likelihood of satisfying this constraint by random generation seems low. Alternatively, if complete coverage is achieved then it is likely to have generated a large number of test cases. The checking of the output from the execution would require an impractically high level of human effort.

Intuitively, random testing would appear to be of little practical value. Results from some recent studies counter this view [Dur81, Dur84, Loo88].

Adaptive perturbation testing is based on assessing the effectiveness of a set of test cases. The effectiveness measure is used to generate further test cases with the aim of increasing the effectiveness. Both Cooper and Andrews [Coo76, And79] describe systems which undertake this automatically for the testing of real-time systems.

Table 2.2 *A decision table used for testing.*

		1	2	3	4	5	6	7	8
c1	*char*1 = 'A'	y	y	y	y	n	n	n	n
c2	*char*1 = 'B'	y	y	n	n	y	y	n	n
c3	*char*2 numeric	y	n	y	n	y	n	y	n
70	make update			x		x			
71	message *M*1							x	x
72	message *M*2				x		x		x
	impossible case	x	x						

The cornerstone of the technique is the use of executable assertions. The software developer inserts assertions into the software. The aim is then to maximize the number of assertion violations. An initial set of test cases is provided by the tester; this is executed and the assertion violations recorded. Each test case is now considered in turn. The single input parameter of the test case that contributes least to the assertion violation count is identified. Optimization routines are then used to find the best value to replace the discarded value such that the number of assertion violations is maximized. The test case is said to have undergone perturbation. This is repeated for each test case. The perturbed set of test cases are executed and the cycle is repeated until the number of violated assertions can be increased no further.

Decision tables and cause-effect graphing based testing is a technique normally employed during system and acceptance testing. The strength of this approach to test data selection lies in its exploration of the combinations of input values. Goodenough and Gerhart [Goo75] and Myers [Mye79] suggest the use of decision tables as a means of developing test cases based on a reading of the specification. Consider the following simple specification for a validation program:

- The first character must be an 'A' or a 'B'.
- The second character must be numeric.
- When these two conditions are satisfied update the file.
- When the first character is incorrect message *M1* is given.
- When the second character is incorrect message *M2* is given.

A decision table for representing the test cases required for this specification is given as Table 2.2. The first two cases are impossible because the first character cannot be both 'A' and 'B' simultaneously and hence can be discounted.

The construction of decision tables directly from specifications for large programs normally results in exceedingly large tables containing many impossible cases. To avoid this Myers [Mye79] advocates the use of a cause-effect graph which employs only the Boolean logical operators $\vee$, $\wedge$ and $\neg$ as an intermediate notation between a requirements specification and a decision table. He has described a series of steps for determining cases using cause-effect graphs and decision tables:

- Divide the specification into workable pieces. A workable piece might be the specification for an individual transaction. This step is necessary because a cause-effect graph for a whole system would be too unwieldy for practical use.

- Identify causes and effects. A cause is an input stimulus; for example an input variable, and an effect is an output response.

- Construct a graph to link the causes and effects in a way that represents the semantics of the specification. This is the cause-effect graph.

- Annotate the graph to show impossible effects and impossible combinations of causes.

- Convert the graph into a decision table. Conditions represent the causes, actions represent the effects and rules represent the test cases.

Figure 2.2 shows a cause-effect graph for the example specification shown on page 18. Note the relationship marked 'e'. This shows a constraint between C1 and C2 , in this case one of exclusivity. Only one of C1 and C2 can be true at one instant–though both may be false.

Having constructed the cause-effect graph it is now used to develop a decision table. This is done by working from each effect and tracing back through the graph finding all combinations of causes that will yield the effect and all combinations that will not. Each combination requires a test to be included in the decision table. Consideration of the constraints bars the inclusion of impossible test cases.

In a simple case, such as the one above with 3 conditions, it is tempting to feel that the cause-effect graph is an unnecessary intermediate representation. However, Myers [Mye79] illustrates the creation of test cases for a specification containing 18 causes. To progress immediately to the decision table would give 262 144 potential test cases. This is a graphic indication that the purpose of the cause-effect graph is to identify the small number of useful test cases.

2.1.6 Dynamic-structural

Here the software is executed with test cases. Creation of the test cases is generally based upon some analysis of the software.

Domain and computation testing are strategies for selecting test cases. They use the structure of the program and select paths which are

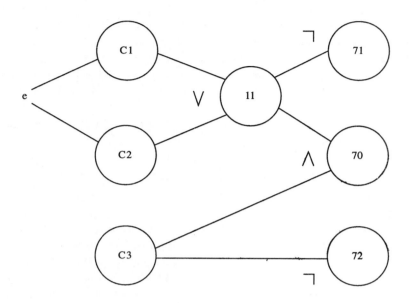

Figure 2.2 *A cause-effect graph.*

used to identify domains. The assignment statements on the paths are used
to consider the computations on the path. Both these approaches also make
use of the ideas of symbolic execution and path computation.

A **path computation** is a set of algebraic expressions–one for each
output variable–expressed in terms of input variables and constants for a
particular path. A **path condition** is the conjunction of constraints on
the path. A **path domain** is the set of input values that satisfy the path
condition. An empty path domain means that the path is infeasible and
cannot be executed.

The class of error that result when a case follows the wrong path due to
a fault in a conditional statement is termed a **domain error**. The class
of error that results when a case correctly follows a path which contains
faults in an assignment statement is termed a **computation error**.

Domain testing is based on the observation that points satisfying boundary conditions are most sensitive to domain errors, for example, a programmer writing a > operator when a ≥ operator is needed [Cla83]. A domain
testing strategy selects test data on and near the boundaries of each path

domain [Whi80, Wey80]. In contrast, computation testing strategies are aimed at the detection of computation errors; here test data for which the path is sensitive to computation errors are selected by analysing the symbolic representation of the path computation [Cla83].

Automated test generation occurs when software is to be executed and the aim is to achieve a particular level of coverage indicated by a coverage metric. Some of the earliest forms of automatic test data generators (ATDGs) used in the computer industry produced random values for input variables based on the simple use of random number generators.

It has been suggested that test data can be generated from a syntactic description of the test data expressed in, say, BNF [Inc85]. This may seem a novel idea as it is not usual to prepare such a syntactic description of the data, but it is a technique familiar to compiler writers [Baz82, Han70, Pay78]. In the case of compilers a carefully prepared data description, that of the programming language, is available. The principle may be transferable to test data generation in general.

Many ATDGs have used the approach of path identification and symbolic execution to aid the data generation process for example CASEGEN [Ram76] and the FORTRAN testbed [Hed81]. The system of predicates produced for a path is part-way to generating test data. If the path predicates cannot be solved due to a contradiction, then the path is infeasible. Any solution of these predicates will provide a series of data values for the input variables, thus providing a test case.

Repeated use of the path generation and predicate solving parts of such a system may produce a set of test cases in which there is a confidence of a high structural coverage of the program. The initial path generation will provide the highest coverage. Subsequent attempts to find feasible paths which incorporate remaining uncovered statements, branches and LCSAJs normally prove increasingly difficult, and in some cases impossible.

A path-based approach which does not use symbolic execution is incorporated in the SMOTL system [Bic79] which has a novel approach to minimizing the number of paths required to achieve full branch coverage.

A program that has been tested with a high coverage may still not meet its specification. This may be due to the omission in the program of one of the functions defined in the specification. Consequently, data that is generated from the specification would prove useful in determining such omissions. To achieve this automatically requires a rigorous means of specification. The increasing use of formal specification methods may provide the necessary foundations on which to build automated functional test data generators.

Mutation analysis is not concerned with creating test data, nor of demonstrating that the program is correct. It is concerned with the quality of a set of test data [Bud78, Bud80] and involves the generation of large numbers of versions of the software under test with artificial errors inserted.

While other forms of testing use the test data to test the program, mutation analysis uses the program to test the test data.

The inclusion of mutation analysis as a dynamic-structural technique perhaps reduces the homogeneity of the class, because it does not focus on how the cases were created but is concerned with assessing the quality of the test cases. Nevertheless, its inclusion in this class of testing methods can be justified because it executes the software and makes some consideration of the software in that a change is applied.

High quality test data will harshly exercise a program. To provide a measure of how well the program has been exercised, mutation analysis creates a large number of almost identical programs. These programs are termed *mutants* where one change is made per mutant. Each mutant program and the original program are executed with the same set of test data. The output from the original program is compared with the output from each mutant in turn. If the outputs are different, then that particular mutant is of little interest as the test data has discovered that there is a difference between the programs. This mutant is now deemed to have been 'killed' and disregarded. A mutant which produces output that matches with the original is interesting. The change has not been detected by the test data, and the mutant is said to be 'live'.

Once the output from all the mutants has been examined a ratio of killed to live mutants will be available to the tester. A high proportion of live mutants indicates a poor set of test data. A further set of test data must be devised and the process repeated until the number of live mutants is small, indicating that the program has been well tested.

A difficulty for mutation analysis occurs when a mutant program is an equivalent program to the original program. Although the mutant is textually different from the original it will always produce the same results as the original program. Mutation analysis will record this as a 'live' mutant, even though no test data can be devised to kill it. The difficulty lies in the fact that determining the state of equivalence is, in general, unsolvable and hence cannot be taken into account when assessing the ratio of live to killed mutants.

Mutation analysis relies on the notion that if test data discovers the single change that has been made to produce the mutant, then the test data will discover more major faults in the program. Thus, if the test data has not discovered any major faults and a high proportion of the mutants have been killed, then the program is likely to be sound.

2.2 Effectiveness of program testing techniques

If the use of a program testing technique is guaranteed to always reveal the presence of a particular error in a program, then the technique is termed to be **reliable** for the error [How78b]. While much work has been undertaken to develop new approaches to testing, only a few researchers have attempted to determine the effectiveness and reliability of existing program testing techniques [How78b, Hen83, Bas87].

2.2.1 Howden's study

One of the first sets of empirical data on testing techniques was provided by a study carried out by Howden [How78b] who tested six programs of various types using several different testing techniques. The techniques assessed were: path testing, branch testing functional structured testing, integrated structured testing, special values testing, anomaly analysis, special requirements testing, interface analysis and symbolic testing.

The first five of these techniques are dynamic-structural approaches to testing. Path and branch testing are used here to mean executing all paths and all branches respectively at least once. Structured testing is an attempt to approximate to path testing which is usually impossible because of the large, if not infinite, number of paths. Programs are decomposed into a hierarchy of functional modules and all paths through a module which require two or less iterations of each loop are tested at least once.

Functional structured testing assesses an individual module, while integrated structured testing treats each module in the context of the whole program. Special values testing is the act of testing a program with cases known to be problematic; for example, string processing programs being tested with empty strings.

The last four techniques are static approaches to testing. Path anomaly analysis is the examination of a program for suspicious looking features such as referencing a variable that has not been assigned a value. Special requirements testing involves checking that the specification stipulates the processing to be applied to all of the input domain dictated by the type of the input variables. Interface analysis is the checking of the consistency of the calling and called parameter lists. Symbolic testing symbolically executes paths. Here, the output is used in two ways. First, it is used simply to generate expressions for the output variables and the path condition. Second, it is used to help generate test data which is then executed.

The generation of test cases and the static analyses were undertaken by hand but, because the use of the techniques require the application of well defined rules rather than the making of skill-based decisions, the results are repeatable. The results of the analysis are shown in Table 2.3. Howden gives eight examples of errors to illustrate the differing combinations of techniques that will discover different classes of error. Table 2.4 summarizes Howden's comments on the effectiveness of each technique for each of the eight example errors. A blank entry indicates that no comment was made about the technique's ability to discover the error, Y indicates success and N indicates that the technique was unable to discover the error.

Table 2.3 *Results of Howden's experiment.*

Program	A	B	C	D	E	F	Total
No. of errors present	3	20	1	2	1	1	28
No. of errors found							
Paths	2	12	1	2	1	0	18
Branches	3	3	0	0	0	0	6
Functional structured	2	5	1	2	0	0	10
Integrated structured	3	6	1	2	0	0	12
Combined structured	3	6	1	2	0	0	12
Special values	3	10	1	2	1	0	17
Anomaly analysis	2	2	0	0	0	0	4
Special requirements	0	4	1	2	0	0	7
Interface analysis	0	2	0	0	0	0	2
Symbolic expression	2	11	1	2	1	0	17
All	3	19	1	2	1	0	26

Table 2.4 *Summary of Howden's analysis.*

Error	1	2	3	4	5	6	7	8
Paths				N		N	N	
Branches	N			N		N	N	
Functional structured				N		N	N	
Integrated structured				N		N	N	
Combined structured	Y	N	N	N	N	N	N	N
Special values		Y		N	Y	N	N	
Anomaly analysis			Y	N		N	N	
Special requirements				Y		N	Y	
Interface analysis				N		N	N	Y
Symbolic expressions				N	Y	Y	N	Y

Unfortunately, no mention is made of the two errors that could not be detected by any of the techniques. Insufficient data is provided to establish which combinations of the techniques are sufficient on their own to discover most of the errors.

The results are encouraging for the use of symbolically executed expressions for output variables. Out of a total of 28 errors five were discovered where it would be 'possible for the incorrect variable to take on the values of the correct variable during testing on actual data, thus hiding the presence of the error' [How78b]. Howden concluded that the testing strategy most likely to produce reliable software was one that made use of a variety

Table 2.5 *Test coverage for a COBOL program.*

	TER1%	TER2%	TER3%
TD1	78.6	63.6	40.6
TD2	96.4	88.9	64.0
TD3	97.8	91.3	65.8
TD4	98.0	92.6	67.1
TD5	98.6	93.0	67.4
TD6	99.0	93.8	68.0
TD7	99.4	94.7	68.6
TD8	100.0	97.1	71.7
TD9	100.0	97.5	72.4

of techniques. Unfortunately, no particular set of techniques was proposed, and it was suggested that further research is required to determine the best combination of techniques for particular circumstances.

2.2.2 Hennell, Hedley and Riddell's study

Hennell *et al.* [Hen83] undertook a study to assess the effectiveness of the LDRA testbed in finding faults in an already working system which had previously been tested by *ad hoc* methods. In the two experiments the LDRA testbed discovered errors not discovered by previous testing.

The testbed measures three coverage metrics TER1, TER2 and TER3 which characterise the percentage of statements, branches and LCSAJs respectively that have been covered by the testing.

Tables 2.5 and 2.6 show the coverage of statements, branches and LC-SAJs attained. Entry TD1 indicates the results for the best functional test data entries; TD2 and TD3 are further tests which were executed to give acceptable cover. These tests found 33 errors in the two programs not detected by previous *ad hoc* testing. Table 2.7 shows the errors classified into 13 fault classes. Unfortunately, but perhaps not surprisingly, the authors experienced difficulty in attributing the detection of the errors to TER1, TER2 and TER3. The authors concluded that after many years in attempting to quantify the testing process, satisfying TER3 = 100% in conjunction with a functional test set is the most cost-effective method of finding errors. However, they do not provide a sufficient explanation.

2.2.3 Basili and Selby's study

Basili and Selby's study [Bas87] involved experiments to determine how testing effectiveness relates to several factors such as testing technique,

Table 2.6 *Test coverage for a PL/1 program.*

	TER1%	TER2%	TER3%
TD1	61.5	47.9	37.5
TD2	73.5	63.5	50.7
TD3	78.2	68.9	55.4
TD4	83.6	76.5	62.5
TD5	88.0	81.5	70.0
TD6	90.9	87.0	75.1
TD7	91.3	87.4	76.1

Table 2.7 *Analysis of errors from Hennel's experiment.*

Error	Number
Initialisation error	2
Single statement error	3
Two uncoupled single statement errors	1
Missing loop	2
Compensating loop errors	2
Incorrect predicate	1
Compensating loop and alternates	1
Alternate missing in nested loops	2
Alternate missing in nesting alternates in a loop	6
Loop missing in nested alternates in a loop	1
Combinatorial error from nested alternates	3
Combination between nested loops	1
None of the above	5

software type, fault type, tester experience, and any interaction among these factors.

The testing techniques examined were: functional testing, in particular equivalence class partitioning and boundary value analysis; structural testing using 100% statement coverage; and code reading.

The study examined three different aspects of software testing: fault detection effectiveness, fault detection cost, and classes of fault detected. The results are shown in Table 2.8. An error of omission is where a programmer forgot to insert something into a program; an error of commission is where an error was created in a program, for example, the use of a $<$ operator instead of a $\leq$ operator.

The experimental design used in the final phase of the experiment was a fractional factorial analysis of variance design. This allowed assessment of the three main effects: testing technique, software type, and level of

Table 2.8 *Distribution of faults in Basili's experiment.*

	Omission	Commission	Total
Initialisation	0	2	2
Computation	4	4	8
Control	2	5	7
Interface	2	11	13
Data	2	1	3
Cosmetic	0	1	1
Total	10	24	34

expertise. It also allowed an assessment of the interactions between these effects. The design also measured several dependent variables: percentage of faults detected, time taken, and some on-line measures such as the number of executions of programs.

The main results of this study were:

- The professional programmers who were studied and who used code reading detected more software faults and had a higher fault detection rate than did functional or structural testing; while functional testing detected more faults than did structural testing However, functional and structural testing were not different in fault detection rate.[†]

- In one group of junior and intermediate level programmers, code reading and functional testing did not differ with respect to faults found, but were both superior to structural testing; while in another similar group there was no evident difference between the techniques.

- With the junior and intermediate staff, the effect of the three techniques was not different in fault detection rate.

- The number of faults observed, the fault detection rate and the total effort in detection depended on the type of software tested.

- Code reading detected more interface faults than did the other methods.

- Functional testing detected more control faults than did the other methods.

- When asked to estimate the percentage of faults detected, the staff who carried out code reading gave the most accurate estimates, while those who used functional testing gave the least accurate estimates.

The authors also reported that 'there were few significant interactions between the main effects of testing technique, program and expertise level'.

[†] The authors defined fault detection rate as the number of faults discovered divided by the time spent looking for them.

2.2.4 Summary of empirical data on effectiveness of testing techniques

The main conclusions arising from analysing the empirical data that exists is that the use of a variety of testing techniques is likely to be more effective than the use of a single technique. However, it is not clear whether all the techniques described in this chapter need to be used to discover every fault, or whether there are sets of compatible techniques which, when used together, are likely to discover all of the faults.

The results produced so far are also limited to a few comparatively small studies. These need validating by many more repeated studies along similar lines.

2.3 The evaluation of testing techniques

2.3.1 Classifying evaluation techniques

Approaches to the evaluation of testing techniques may be ordered according to the degree of observation, experimentation, and theoretical evaluation involved. At one end of the scale lies a theoretical approach that makes no use of sample programs or of human testers. In the middle sits the laboratory experiment involving many well-understood sample programs and many subjects whose abilities are known. At the other end is the observational study of real situations over a long period. The three studies described above are at different points on the theoretical-experimental-observational spectrum.

The study by Howden is the nearest to the theoretical end of the spectrum: no human testers were involved. A theoretically perfect-application of the techniques under evaluation was undertaken by the evaluator. Six programs with known errors were used. Had a classification of errors been used to determine which of the techniques is capable of detecting each error, then the approach would have been entirely theoretical.

The study by Basili and Selby is the closest to the experimental midpoint. Many human testers were set the task of testing four quite different programs each containing a set of known errors.

The study by Hennell, *et al.* is the nearest of the three to the observational end. Two production programs were tested by regular users of a testing tool. This study is, however, a long way from the end of the spectrum as the testing was not undertaken as a normal part of the software's development but as a special experiment.

The main shortcoming of the studies undertaken to date is their small number and, consequently, a resulting shortage of data. Basil and Selby's study appears to be a sound experimental design, but it avoids the thorny problem of the differences between the laboratory experiment and the live software development environment. Ideally, this study should have been expanded to include a larger number of software testers; assessing 'real' programs and covering more testing techniques. This would have provided valuable information about which combination of techniques would be the most appropriate for use in testing particular types of software using staff having particular levels of experience. Such a study would, of course, have taken a very long time and be would have been very expensive.

2.3.2 Evaluation of testing techniques: the ideal

There are effectively three approaches to the evaluation of testing techniques: observation, experiment and theory.

An observational study requires the researcher to identify, for each technique to be assessed, several organizations that currently use the technique as part of their normal software development. Over a long period, the development of software is monitored and details of every fault discovered at every stage of the life of the software are recorded. The aim of the analysis would be to assess the number of errors discovered during development using the techniques under investigation and to compare this to the number of errors detected later in the software product's life. This would tell us which technique detects the most errors early in the life of the software. By recording details of software type, experience of user and effort expended assessment can be made of the most cost-effective method.

An experimental study should follow the same design as the study carried out by Basili and Selby. It would assess more testing techniques using more testers from a wider variety of organizations. The main aim of this study would be to gather more data to corroborate the findings of Basili and Selby. Indeed, there would be much to be gained from simply repeating their experiment with different subjects in other environments.

A theoretical study would commence by establishing or selecting a classification of software faults such as those proposed by Van Tassel [Van78] and Kaner [Kan93]. A set of programs is then constructed or identified which contain all the faults listed in the classification. The evaluation would then assess which of the techniques discovered the existence of what type of faults. A weakness of this approach is that it would be difficult to assess the cost-effectiveness of the techniques.

2.4 Summary

The principal objective of software testing is to gain confidence in the software. This requires the discovery of both errors of omission and commission. Confidence arises from thorough testing; happily, there are many techniques which help to achieve thorough testing.

Testing techniques can be assessed according to where along the two main testing strategy dimensions they fall. The first dimension, the functional-structural dimension, assesses the extent to which the function description in the specification, as opposed to the detailed design of the software, is used as a basis for testing. The second dimension, the static-dynamic dimension, considers the degree to which the technique executes the software and assesses its run-time behaviour, as opposed to inferring its run-time behaviour from an examination of program code. These two dimensions can be used to produce four categories of testing techniques: static-functional, static-structural, dynamic-functional and dynamic-structural. As with all classifications this one is problematic at the boundaries: some techniques appear to belong equally well in two categories.

The aims of testing techniques range from demonstrating correctness for all input classes, to showing that for a particular set of test cases no faults were discovered. Debate continues as to whether correctness can be proved for life-size software and about what can be inferred when a set of test cases finds no errors. A major question facing dynamic testing techniques is whether the execution of a single case demonstrates anything more than that the software works for that particular case. This has led to work on the identification of domains, leading to the assertion that a test case represents a particular domain of possible test cases.

Many structural techniques rely on the generation of paths through program code. These techniques are hampered by the lack of a sensible path generation strategy. There is no clear notion of what constitutes a 'revealing' path worthy of investigation as opposed to a 'concealing' path which tells the tester very little.

Testers often utilize their experience of classes of faults associated with particular functions and data types to create additional test cases. To date there is no formal way of taking account of these heuristics.

A significant feature of the little empirical data that has been collected is that use of a variety of testing techniques is likely to detect more errors than reliance upon a single technique.

Symbolic execution looks to be a promising technique. In an experiment Howden [How78b] discovered that symbolic execution was able to discover faults that other techniques would have missed. Yet, few full symbolic execution systems currently exist. It is this topic which the remainder of this book addresses.

CHAPTER 3

The principles of symbolic execution

3.1 Introduction

Symbolic execution creates a set of values for the input variables to a program. The novelty of the technique lies in the nature of the values. Rather than create a set of actual values a set of symbolic values are produced.

In order to illustrate this consider the following program fragment which determines a *netpay*.

```
accept GrossPay
accept TaxPcent
accept TaxFree
compute Taxable = GrossPay − TaxFree
compute NetPay = GrossPay − (Taxable * TaxPcent/100)
display NetPay
```

For each of the input variables the symbolic values are shown in Table 3.1. After symbolically executing the program the value of *NetPay* would be: $g - (g - tf) * pc/100$. This expression not only holds for, say, the numeric values of 600, 25 and 200 for g, pc and tf respectively, but it also represents a general set of values: it represents a domain of test cases.

3.2 Symbolic evaluation

Clarke and Richardson [Cla81] use the phrase 'symbolic evaluation' as a collective title for techniques that make use of algebraic expressions to represent the values of variables. There are three types of symbolic evaluation

Table 3.1 *Values for symbolic execution.*

Input variable	Symbolic value
grosspay	g
taxpcent	pc
taxfree	tf

identified by Clarke and Richardson: simple symbolic execution, dynamic symbolic evaluation and global symbolic evaluation.

3.2.1 Simple symbolic execution

This is the evaluation of a single path using symbolic values. The output from the symbolic execution has two components. The first is a set of expressions in terms of the symbolic values of the input variables and constants. The second is a set of constraints which must be satisfied in order for the path to be executable. Collectively these constraints are known as the **path condition**. There are two approaches to deriving the symbolic expressions and path condition: forward expansion and backward substitution. These are described later in this chapter.

3.2.2 Dynamic symbolic evaluation

Here symbolic execution takes place in parallel with the execution of actual values for variables. For each variable encountered both the actual value and a symbolic expression are maintained. No feasibility checking of the path condition is required as the execution of the actual value case ensures that the path followed is executable unless, of course, a run-time error is produced.

Dynamic symbolic evaluation is normally used for debugging. In addition, user inserted assertions (Boolean expressions) may be checked to see whether the processing of the input case complies with a particular assertion at that point in the path.

3.2.3 Global symbolic evaluation

The aim of global symbolic evaluation is to derive a representation for a whole piece of software–normally a module or a program. Whereas symbolic execution produces a representation of a single path in terms of its input variables and constants, global symbolic evaluation aims to achieve representations for all paths through a routine.

Where a routine contains only one path (no conditional statements) the result is identical to symbolic execution. If conditional statements are present, then a set of path conditions and variable expressions are produced. When a routine contains loops then there is potentially an infinite number of paths. A main aim of global symbolic evaluation is to identify a loop expression. From this expression, further expressions representing successive iterations may be derived providing recurrence relations in terms of the values of variables at successive iterations.

The next step of global symbolic execution involves a loop analysis to solve the recurrence relations. As a result many paths representing differing numbers of iterations of a loop are represented by a single expression. Clarke and Richardson state that 'this is not always straightforward and sometimes may not be possible ... In particular, the dependence may be cyclic–V may be mapped on W, which depends on V–in which case the recurrence relations cannot be solved'. Howden [How78b] has demonstrated that, in general, such recurrence relations cannot be solved and in doing so pointed out that global symbolic evaluation has a bleak future.

Of these three classes of symbolic evaluation this book describes simple symbolic execution.

3.3 An example of simple symbolic execution

Before describing symbolic execution of a path it is useful to introduce the flowgraph representation of a program. This is a useful way of displaying the program's structure. It consists of nodes joined by arcs. The nodes represent branch points within the program and the arcs represent statements that modify variables. The COBOL program* in Figure 3.1 accepts three integers that are interpreted as lengths of the sides of a triangle. It then determines the type of triangle that the values represent and calculates the area of the triangle. The program can be represented by the flowgraph shown in Figure 3.2. A node on the graph corresponds to a selection statement in the program and an arc on the graph corresponds to a series of input, assignment and output statements. The flowgraph contains 33 paths. Symbolic execution considers a single path at a time. There are two approaches to symbolic execution of a path: forward expansion and backward substitution.

3.3.1 Forward expansion

A common form of symbolic execution is known as *forward expansion*. Forward expansion is similar to the normal execution of a path. A path consists of a series of input statements, condition predicates and assignment statements. The symbolic execution commences at the root of the path and proceeds, branch by branch, to the end of the path. During a path traversal each input variable is given a symbolic rather than an actual value. Thereafter, each assignment statement is evaluated so that it is expressed in terms of symbolic values of input variables and constants.

At the end of the symbolic execution of a path the output variables will be represented by expressions in terms of symbolic values of input variables and constants. The output expressions are subject to constraints. The path condition for a path that has been executed is provided by the set of symbolic representations of each condition predicate along the path.

---

* Interested readers can find a brief description of the language used in Appendix A

```
identification division.
program-id. triangle.
data division.
working-storage section.
01 I        pic 9.
01 J        pic 9.
01 K        pic 9.
01 A        pic 9.
01 B        pic 9.
01 C        pic 9.
01 S        pic 9.
01 match    pic 9.
01 area     pic 9.
begin-triangle.
accept I,J,K
if I + J > K ∧ J + K > I ∧ K + I > J
then
    move 0 to match
    compute S = (I + J + K)/2
    compute A = S − I
    compute B = S − J
    compute C = S − K
    compute area = (S * A * B * C) * *0.5
    if  I = J
    then
        add 1 to match
    end-if
    if J = K
    then
        add 1 to match
    end-if
    if  K = I
    then
        add 1 to match
    end-if
    evaluate true
        match = 0: display 'Scalene'
        match = 1: display 'Isosceles'
        match = 3: display 'Equilateral'
        other display 'Error'
    end-evaluate
    display area
else
    display 'Not a Triangle'
end-if
stop run
end program triangle.
```

Figure 3.1 *A triangle program.*

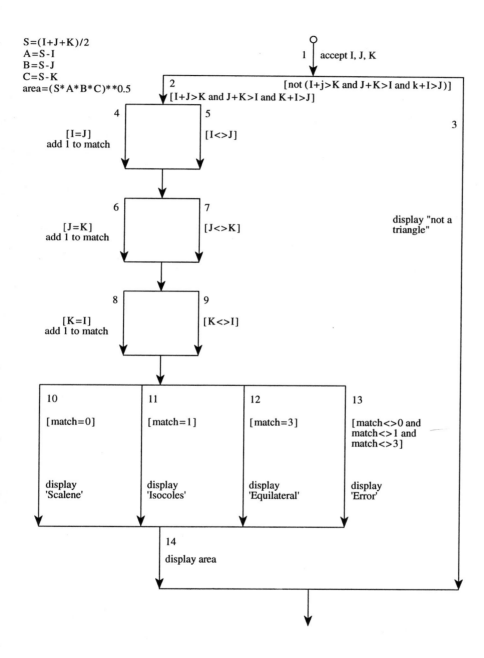

Figure 3.2 *The flow graph of the triangle program.*

Analysis of these constraints may indicate that the path is not executable due to a contradiction.

For each path, a path condition is maintained together with a table containing each variable referenced and a corresponding expression. Initially, each variable expression is empty. As symbolic execution proceeds along a path four categories of statement are identified: input, assignment, predicate, and output. When an input statement is encountered a new symbolic value is created and replaces the current expression representing the variable.

When an assignment is encountered two substitutions take place. First, the variables in the right hand side of the assignment statement are substituted by their current expressions. Second, the resulting assignment expression is used to update the expression representing the target variable. For example, when the assignment is compute $A = B + C$. B and C are replaced by their current expressions say $X + Y$ and $J + K$ giving compute $A = X + Y + J + K$. Third, the current expression for A is replaced by the newly created expression.

When a predicate is encountered each variable in the predicate is substituted by its current expression. Then the predicate is tested for its truth value. When true, for example $A = A$, then it is ignored because it has no impact on the path condition. When false, for example $A \neq A$ the symbolic execution halts because a contradiction has been discovered. When its truth is indeterminate, for example, $A = B$ then the predicate is conjoined to the path condition. When an output is encountered the current expression is displayed.

To illustrate symbolic execution by forward expansion consider the path covering branches (arcs) 1, 2, 4, 6, 8, 12 and 14 of the triangle program. The branches can be written in sequence to isolate the path into a straight-line form, where predicates are enclosed in square brackets. This is shown in Figure 3.3. Symbolic execution of this path is now described.

The current expression for a variable is shown as:

variable: expression

for example, *total* : 0 indicates that the current expression for *total* is 0. The path condition is shown in a similar way. When an execution of a statement is described or a condition compared during execution we shall precede the text that describes this with three asterisks to distinguish it from the surrounding mathematics.

*** 1 accept IJK

this is an input statement so the expressions for I, J and K are given new symbolic values $I : i, J : j, K : k$.

*** 2 $[I + J > K \wedge J + K > I \wedge K + I > J]$

```
1     accept I, J, K
2     [I + J > K ∧ J + K > I ∧ K + I > J]
      move 0 to match
      compute S = (I + J + K)/2
      compute A = S − I
      compute B = S − J
      compute C = S − K
      compute area = (S * A * B * C) * *0.5
4     [I = J]
      add 1 to match
6     [J = K]
      add 1 to match
8     [K = I]
      add 1 to match
12    [match = 3]
      display 'Equilateral'
14    display area
```

Figure 3.3 *Path execution of the triangle programme.*

To progress beyond this point the test case must satisfy the predicate enclosed within the brackets. First, substitute I, J and K by their current expressions. $i + j > k \wedge j + k > i \wedge k + i > j$. Second, decide whether its truth can be determined–no. Third, conjoin it to the path condition which was initially true. The path condition becomes

$$PC : i + j > k \wedge j + k > i \wedge k + i > j$$

*** move 0 to *match*

This is an assignment so the expression for *match* is replaced by 0 hence *match*: 0.

*** compute $S = (I + J + K)/2$

When a variable is assigned the value of an expression the variables that are incorporated in the expression are substituted by their current symbolic expression. In the case of I, J and K their current symbolic values are i, j and k. Thus, $S : (i + j + k)/2$ holds

*** compute $A = S − I$

The symbolic value of A is calculated by substituting the variables on the right-hand-side by their current symbolic values. Thus $A : (i + j + k)/2 − i$ holds.

*** compute $B = S - J$

At this point in the execution $B : (i + j + k)/2 - j$ holds.

*** compute $C = S - K$

At this point in the execution $C : (i + j + k)/2 - k$ holds.

*** compute $area = (S * A * B * C) * *0.5$

At this point in the computation the variable *area* has the symbolic expression

$$\sqrt{t1 * t2 * t3 * t4}$$

where

$$
\begin{aligned}
t1 &= (i + j + k)/2 \\
t2 &= ((i + j + k)/2 - i) \\
t3 &= ((i + j + k)/2 - j) \\
t4 &= (i + j + k)/2 - k)
\end{aligned}
$$

The next statement to be executed is

*** 4 $[I = J]$

$i = j$ is conjoined to the path condition. This becomes

$$PC : i + j > k \wedge j + k > i \wedge k + i > j \wedge i = j$$

The path condition may be simplified (but this is not essential) to:

$$PC : i = j \wedge 2 * i > k \wedge k > 0$$

The next execution is

*** add 1 to *match*

here *match* is incremented by 1 and hence *match* : 1

*** 6 $[J = K]$

$j = k$ is conjoined to the path condition giving

$$PC : i = j \wedge 2 * i > k \wedge k > 0 \wedge j = k$$

simplifying this gives:

$$PC : i = j \wedge j = k \wedge k > 0$$

The next statement to be symbolically executed is

*** add 1 to *match*

   Hence, *match* : 2 now holds

8   $[K = I]$

$k = i$ is conjoined to the PC which becomes

$$PC : i = j \land j = k \land k > 0 \land k = i$$

Simplifying merely removes the added constraint $k = i$ and hence PC:$i = j \land j = k \land k > 0$ holds.

add 1 **to** *match*

At this point *match* : 3 holds.

*** 12   [*match* = 3]

match is substituted with its current expression. At this point $3 = 3$ This is true so the predicate is ignored.

*** display 'Equilateral'

The output string is noted

*** 14   **display** *area*

The output expression is noted. At the end of symbolic execution of the path the following inputs and outputs have been identified.
Inputs: $I = i, J = j, K = k$

Output: 'Equilateral'

$$area = \sqrt{(t1 * t2 * t3 * t4}$$

where

$$
\begin{aligned}
t1 &= (i + j + k)/2 \\
t2 &= ((i + j + k)/2 - i) \\
t3 &= ((i + j + k)/2 - j) \\
t4 &= (i + j + k)/2 - k)
\end{aligned}
$$

The path condition is

PC: $i = j \land j = k \land k > 0$

The path condition dictates that output of the string 'Equilateral' will result when $i = j = k > 0$. This matches with expectation. It is not so straightforward to verify that the output for 'area' is correct. This is most easily achieved by substituting i, j and k with values, evaluating the expression and comparing the result against an earlier calculation of the result for the chosen values.

The path considered above is feasible, but some paths chosen through a program are likely to be infeasible. As an illustration of symbolically executing an infeasible path by forward expansion consider the path 1, 2, 4, 7, 8, 13 and 14.

The branches of this path are as follows:

1 accept I, J, K
2 $[I + J > K \wedge J + K > I \wedge K + I > J]$
  move 0 to *match*
  compute $s = (I + J + K)/2$
  compute $a = S - I$
  compute $b = S - J$
  compute $c = S - K$
  compute $area = (S * A * B * C) * *0.5$
4 $[I = J]$
  add 1 to *match*
7 $[J \neq K]$
8 $[K = I]$
  add 1 to *match*
13 $[match \neq 0 \wedge match \neq 1 \wedge match \neq 3]$
  display 'Error'
14 display *area*

Symbolic execution of this path is shown below

*** 1 accept I, J, K

At this point $I : i, J : i, K : k$ holds.

*** 2 $[I + J > K \wedge J + K > I \wedge K + I > J]$

The path condition is

$$PC : i + j > k \wedge j + k > i \wedge k + i > j$$

*** move 0 to *match*

At this point *match* : 0 holds.

*** compute $s = (I + J + K)/2$

At this point $S : (i + j + k)/2$ holds.

*** compute a = S-I

At this point $A : (i + j + k)/2 - i$ holds.

*** compute $b = S - J$

At this point in the execution $B : (i + j + k)/2 - j$ holds.

*** compute $c = S - K$

At this point in the execution $C : (i + j + k)/2 - k$ holds.

*** compute $area = (S * A * B * C) * *0.5$

At this point

$$\text{area} : \sqrt{t1 * t2 * t3 * t4}$$

holds. Where

$$
\begin{aligned}
t1 &= (i + j + k)/2 \\
t2 &= ((i + j + k)/2 - i) \\
t3 &= ((i + j + k)/2 - j) \\
t4 &= (i + j + k)/2 - k)
\end{aligned}
$$

*** 4 $[I = J]$

At this point the path the path condition has become

$$\text{PC} : i + j > k \land j + k > i \land k + i > j \land i = j$$

This can be simplified to

$$\text{PC} : i = j \land 2 * i > k \land k > 0$$

*** add 1 to *match*

At this point *match* : 1 holds. To this point the symbolic execution is the same as for the path described earlier.

*** 7 $[J \neq K]$

The path condition becomes

$$\text{PC} : i = j \land 2 * i > k \land k > 0 \land j \neq k$$

*** 8 $[K = I]$

The path condition now becomes

$$\text{PC} : i = j \land 2 * i > k \land k > 0 \land j \neq k \land k = i.$$

Which simplifies to

$$\text{PC} : i = j \land j = k \land j \neq k \land k > 0.$$

This path condition is infeasible. It is not worthwhile continuing the symbolic execution further as it will always remain infeasible.

This approach to symbolic execution is termed 'forward expansion' as the execution commences from the root of the directed graph and progresses through the program from the entry point to an exit point. As the traversal of the path progresses, the path condition is gradually expanded as each condition and relevant variable assignment is encountered. It has the advantage of detecting infeasibility at the point at which the infeasibility first occurs.

3.3.2 Backward substitution

Backward substitution adopts the opposite approach to forward expansion: it starts the symbolic execution of a path from the terminating point of the program as opposed to the starting point.

Backward substitution of a path is a more complicated procedure than forward expansion. It is iterative in nature, repeatedly returning to expressions previously processed. Consider again the feasible path 1, 2, 4, 6, 8, 12 and 14 of the triangle program shown in Figure 3.3 which is now symbolically executed backwards.

*** 14   display *area*

At this point no values have been attributed to the variable *area* but it is important to note the occurrence of each output variable.

*** display 'Equilateral'

Note the output of the string.

*** 12 [*match* = 3]

At this point PC: $match = 3$ holds.

*** add 1 to *match*

As the initial value is not known at this stage the expression must remain in terms of *match*. Thus match : $match + 1$ holds at this point.

*** 8 [*K* = *I*]

At this point the path condition PC : $match = 3 \wedge K = I$ holds.

*** add 1 to *match*

match has already been encountered at branch 12 resulting in an expression which must now be modified. This is achieved by substituting the expression created at branch 12 into the occurrence of *match* on the right hand side of the assignment in branch 8. Thus *match* is substituted by $match + 1$ giving match : $match + 2$.

*** 6   [*J* = *K*]

At this point the path condition is

$$PC : match = 3 \wedge K = I \wedge J = K$$

*** add 1 to *match*

At this point $match : match + 3$ holds.

*** 4 [I=J]

The path condition hence becomes

$$PC : match = 3 \wedge K = I \wedge J = K \wedge K = I$$

this simplifies to

$$PC : match = 3 \wedge K = I \wedge J = K$$

*** compute $area = (S * A * B * C) * *0.5$

This results in $area : (S * A * B * C) * *0.5$ holding.

*** compute $C = S - K$

At this point $C : S - K$ holds. The handling of this assignment illustrates the essence of backward substitution. At each assignment a search must be made through each expression of each previously noted variable for the variable being assigned the new value. When the variable is found in an expression it is substituted by the new expression resulting from the assignment. In this case the previous expression for the variable $area$ must now be modified to take account of the new value of variable C. This means that

$$area : \sqrt{S * A * B * (S - K)}$$

holds.

*** compute $B = S - J$

The following then hold.

$$B : S - J \quad area : \sqrt{S * A * (S - J) * (S - K)}$$

*** compute $A = S - I$

The following then hold

$$A : S - I \quad area : \sqrt{S * (S - I) * (S - J) * (S - K)}$$

*** compute $S = (I + J + K)/2$

Thus, $S : (I + J + K)/2$ now holds. Again $area$ must be modified; so too must A, B and C. This means that $area$ becomes:

$$\sqrt{t1 * t2 * t3 * t4}$$

where

$$
\begin{aligned}
t1 &= (I + J + K)/2 \\
t2 &= ((I + J + K)/2 - I) \\
t3 &= ((I + J + K)/2 - J) \\
t4 &= ((I + J + K)/2 - K)
\end{aligned}
$$

and where the following hold

$$A : (I + J + K)/2 - I \quad B : (I + J + K)/2 - J \quad C : (I + J + K)/2 - K$$

*** move 0 to *match*

The current expression for match is $match : match + 3$. If we substitute 0 in place of *match* in the expression then $match : 3$ holds and the path condition becomes

$$PC : 3 = 3 \land K = I \land J = K$$

which simplifies to

$$PC : K = I \land J = K$$

*** 2 $[I + J > K \land J + K > I \land K + I > J]$

This means that the path condition becomes

$$PC : K = I \land J = K \land I + J > K \land J + K > I \land K + I > J$$

which simplifies to give

$$PC : K = I \land J = K \land I > 0$$

*** 1 accept I, J, K

This gives

$$I : i, J : j, K : k$$
$$\overline{area : \sqrt{t1 * t2 * t3 * t4}}$$
$$A : (i + j + k)/2 - i$$
$$B : (i + j + k)/2 - j$$
$$C : (i + j + k)/2 - k$$

where

$$
\begin{aligned}
t1 &= (i + j + k)/2 \\
t2 &= (i + j + k)/2 - i) \\
t3 &= ((i + j + k)/2 - j) \\
t4 &= (i + j + k)/2 - k)
\end{aligned}
$$

As can be seen the backward substitution approach to symbolic execution yields exactly the same results as forward expansion.

The next illustration is that of the backward substitution of an infeasible path. Consider again the path 1, 2, 4, 7, 8, 13 and 14.

*** 14 display *area*

Note the output variable.

*** display 'Error'

Note the output string.

*** 13   [$match \neq 0 \wedge match \neq 1 \wedge match \neq 3$]

The path condition is then

$$PC : match \neq 0 \wedge match \neq 1 \wedge match \neq 3$$

*** **add** 1 **to** *match*

match : *match* + 1 then holds.

*** 8   [$K = I$]

The path condition at this point becomes

$$PC : match <> 0 \wedge match <> 1 \wedge match <> 3 \wedge K = I.$$

*** 7   [$J <> K$]

and the path condition becomes

$$PC : match \neq 0 \wedge match \neq 1 \wedge match \neq 3 \wedge K = I \wedge J \neq K$$

*** **add** 1 **to** match

hence *match* : *match* + 2 holds.

*** 4   [$I = J$]

The path condition now becomes

$$PC : match \neq 0 \wedge match \neq 1 \wedge match \neq 3 \wedge K = I \wedge J \neq K \wedge I = J$$

At this point the path has become infeasible because J cannot be both equal to K and not equal to K simultaneously.

Ramamoorthy [Ram76] claims that in backward substitution, assignment statements that do not affect any conditional statements need not be symbolically executed. This is not wholly satisfactory. Application of this rule could cause the omission of assignments that affect the expressions of output variables. Four categories of assignment statement can be identified:

- assignments that affect conditional statements and output variables;
- assignments that affect only conditional statements;
- assignments that affect only output variables;
- assignments that affect neither conditional statements nor the output variables.

By application of Ramamoorthy's approach the first two categories are included in the symbolic execution, while the last two categories are excluded. It is the omission of the third category that is of concern. The set of output variable expressions would be incomplete even though the path condition would be accurate. An occurrence of a statement in the fourth category in a program is of interest. If an assignment affects neither output variables nor the path condition then its presence in the program should be questioned.

Ramamoorthy [Ram76] further claims that backward substitution has the benefit of being the simpler operationally and requires the least storage space. However, forward expansion may determine infeasibility more quickly, handles arrays more simply and perhaps, most importantly, is intuitively more obvious than backward substitution. It is these advantages that have led to the more widespread adoption of forward expansion at the expense of backward substitution.

3.4 Simplification of symbolic expressions

The usefulness of the output of symbolic expressions, though potentially helpful, is hampered by the unfamiliar format of the expressions. One possible solution to this difficulty is to attempt to simplify the expression in the hope that it will be more meaningful. By simplifying an expression, evidence is lost of how the expression was calculated. This evidence may prove helpful in pin-pointing a fault in the program. Both the simplified and the unsimplified expressions should be provided as output.

In the above examples of the output from feasible paths the expression for area is expressed as:

$$\sqrt{(i+j+k)/2 * ((i+j+k)/2 - i) * ((i+j+k)/2 - j) * (i+j+k)/2 - k)}$$

This expression could be further simplified to:

$$\sqrt{((i+j+k) * (-i+j+k) * (i-j+k) * (i+j-k))/4}$$

In algebraic terms these two expressions are equivalent. However, a potential difficulty exists when expressions are evaluated using different computers. Execution of the two expressions should give identical outputs, but rounding and truncation of intermediate results could yield slightly different results. This may cause execution of an unintended path to take place.

3.5 Problems in applying symbolic execution

There are four problem areas which are well documented in the literature concerning the application of symbolic execution. These are: path selection and the evaluation of loops; a dilemma over how to process module calls; the evaluation of array references dependent on input values; and the checking of path feasibility. There are three further problems concerning the application of numerical optimizers for checking feasibility which are not documented in the literature; these are described later in the book in Section 4.5.1.

3.5.1 Path selection and loops

Current methods of path selection employ only simple strategies such as taking the true branch first or generating the shortest path. These strategies have a common target: that of achieving a particular coverage metric such as that all statements or all branches are executed at least once. Each of these strategies is sensitive to the problem of selecting infeasible paths.

Having identified a set of paths which cover, say all branches, some of the selected paths will be found to be infeasible. This leaves the problem of identifying feasible paths which include the non-covered branches resulting from the infeasible paths. Further, such a strategy does not consider the usefulness of the selected paths.

Many systems that use symbolic execution have two distinct stages. First, they select a path. Second, they symbolically execute the selected path. Ideally, a symbolic execution testing system should incorporate a path selection strategy in which path selection and symbolic execution take place together. Such co-operative processing allows the expressions produced during symbolic execution to be utilised in path selection in an attempt to select only feasible paths.

Symbolic execution cannot proceed beyond a loop unless the number of iterations is known. The reason for this is that usually inside a loop symbolic expressions will be calculated which depend on the number of iterations. A common strategy for placing loops on paths is to create three paths: one that contains zero iterations of the loop; a second that contains one iteration; and a third containing two iterations. The idea behind this strategy is that zero, one and two iterations coincide with three classes of loop error and so each should be tested. Consider the following loop:

```
perform until x = y
compute x = x + 1
display '- no advancing'
end-perform
```

Assume that x and y are input variables, and that earlier processing has guaranteed that x is less than or equal to y. Three paths would be selected where the following predicates are conjoined to the path condition. This is shown as Table 3.2. These three paths would provide reasonable coverage of the loop.

Consider the following code which produces the Fibonacci series. The program accepts three values; the first two act as commencing values and the third as the number of terms to be displayed.

Table 3.2 *Three loops and path conditions.*

Path number	Number of iterations	Predicates conjoined to path condition
1	0	$x = y$
2	1	$x < y,\ x + 1 = y$
3	2	$x < y,\ x + 1 < y,\ x + 2 = y$

```
1    accept last, this, A
2    move 2 to N
3    display last
4    display this
5    perform until N >= A
6        compute next = last + this
7        move this to last
8        move next to this
9        display next
10       add 1 to N
11   end-perform
```

The important feature of this program with respect to symbolic execution is that the number of iterations of the loop is controlled by the input variable A. To demonstrate the impact of this feature consider the following symbolic execution of the program where the symbolic expressions for the output variables and the state of the path condition are given in the right-hand column.

1	accept *last, this, A*	$A : a, \text{last} : l, \text{this} : t$
2	move 2 to N	$N : 2$
3	display *last*	Output: l
4	display *this*	Output: t
5	$[N >= A]$	PC: $2 >= A$
6	compute *next* = *last* + *this*	next : $l + t$
7	move *this* to *last*	last : t
8	move *next* to *this*	this : $l + t$
9	display *next*	Output: $l + t$
10	add 1 to N	$N : 3$
11	end-perform	
5	$[N >= A]$	PC: $3 >= A$
6	compute *next* = *last* + *this*	next : $l + 2t$
7	move *this* to *last*	last : $l + t$
8	move *next* to *this*	this : $l + 2t$
9	display *next*	Output: $l + 2t$
10	add 1 to N	$N : 4$

```
11   end-perform
5    [N >= A]                            [PC: 4 >= A
6    compute next = last + this         next : 2l + 3t
7    move this to last                  last : l + 2t
8    move next to this                  this : 2l + 3t
9    display next                       Output 2l + 3t
10   add 1 to N                         N : 5
11   end-perform
5    [N >= A]                           PC: 5 >= A
6    compute next = last + this         next : 3l + 5t
7    move this to last                  last : 2l + 3t
8    move next to this                  this : 3l + 5t
9    display next                       Output:3l + 5t
10   add 1 to N                         N : 6
11   end-perform
5    [N >= A]                           PC: 6 >= A
6    compute next = last + this         next : 5l + 8t
7    move this to last                  last : 3l + 5t
8    move next to this                  this : 5l + 8t
9    display next                       Output:5l + 8t
10   add 1 to N                         N : 7
11   end-perform
```

There is no complex recurrence relation to solve here; it is a simple matter to determine that the expression representing the number of iterations is $a - 2$ More complicated loop recurrence relations pose a more severe test for symbolic execution.

Ramamoorthy, Ho and Chen [Ram76] note that, in general, solving such recurrence relations is not a simple task. Cheatham [Che79] reports on an improved technique for solving the more common recurrence relations in which the symbolic expression that describes the number of iterations is produced.

3.5.2 Module calls

The term 'module call' is used here to refer to the invocation of any out-of-line code. This includes sub-programs that are compiled separately from the invoking program, internal sub-routines, procedures and functions. The dilemma concerning module calls is whether to treat them using a macro-expansion approach [Boy75], the lemma approach [Che79, Han76] or using an approach which regards each call as an I/O boundary.

For example, in a COBOL program, when an out-of-line perform is encountered during the symbolic execution of a path the execution may proceed by executing into the performed procedure. This is macro-expansion. Each time the performed paragraph is invoked the symbolic execution will be repeated, starting anew at each invocation. In contrast the lemma approach would symbolically execute a module once, and then use the results produced each time the module is invoked. The adoption of an I/O boundary would cause new values to be assigned to the returned parameters.

A reasonable approach might be to employ macro expansion for internal subroutines where global variables are used, such as the COBOL performed paragraph, and to use the lemma approach where only parameters are passed. When external routines are called, the parameters passed to the invoked routine can be treated as output results and the returned values as input variables which are then given new symbolic values. Each separately compiled program is thus evaluated independently. Parameters passed to and from invoked modules should be regarded as output and input variables respectively. This approach is in keeping with the aims of decomposition: the division of problems into units of manageable proportions and cohesive functions.

3.5.3 Arrays

Arrays can be problematic for symbolic execution [Cla76b, Kin76, Ram76, How77]. There is no difficulty for an expression such as:

move B to $A(5)$

because $A(5)$ is unique in the same sense that B is unique. Both refer to a specific single element; this enables symbolic execution to proceed in the usual way. The difficulty arises when the subscript is an input variable, or is dependent upon at least one input variable, for example:

move B to $A(I)$

where I is an input variable. Symbolic execution cannot proceed in the usual way beyond this assignment, because the identification of the element within the array is not defined and is said to be an ambiguous array element.

One approach replaces array references with an n-way branching construct containing one branch for each array element. For example

move B to $A(I)$

is replaced by

1   move B to $A(1)$
2   move B to $A(2)$
3   move B to $A(3)$
4   move B to $A(4)$

where A is an array with four elements. This approach increases the number of paths substantially, even for small arrays. Where the number of elements in an array is large this approach is impractical.

Alternatively, when the path condition is to be used to derive a test case the ambiguity can persist during symbolic execution and be resolved during the creation of the test case. This approach needs special processing because path infeasibility cannot be assessed in the usual way.

3.5.4 Identifying infeasible paths

Of the 33 paths through the triangle program in Figure 3.1 only 6 are feasible. Symbolic execution must be capable of determining when constraints on a path are contradictory and hence the path is infeasible.

Clarke and Richardson [Cla81] describe two approaches to determining infeasibility: axiomatic and algebraic. The axiomatic technique makes use of a theorem proving system to determine whether the constraints are contradictory. The algebraic technique uses the simple conditions within the path condition as a set of constraints. An artificial objective function is created, for example, the sum of the variables present in the predicates. If this optimization problem can be solved, then the path is feasible. The solution obtained may then be used as a test case to execute the path.

When no solution can be found an indication as to which constraints contribute to the infeasibility would be useful. This is not easily obtained because the algorithms employed do not readily identify the constraint which contributes most to the infeasibility.

A potentially more successful approach might be to submit the first and second constraints on the path to the optimizer for solution. If this proves to be feasible then add the next constraint on the path and attempt to solve. This addition of constraints is repeated until either the path is complete or the constraints are infeasible. This approach identifies the constraint which first causes infeasibility.

An alternative, reverse approach, could also be adopted by attempting to solve for the complete set of path constraints. If the path proves to be infeasible, then the last constraint is removed and a solution attempted for the remaining constraints. Constraints are then removed until a feasible solution is determined.

Another approach is to use binary division. First, attempt to find a solution for the complete path. If this is infeasible, then try a set of constraints for the top (first) half of the path. Continue halving the unknown set of constraints until the offending constraint is determined. This approach, if useful, is likely to be appropriate only for paths with a large number of predicates.

We feel the most useful approach is to combine path selection and symbolic execution, undertaking feasibility assessments after each branch selection is made. If the addition of the selected predicate causes infeasibility an alternative predicate is chosen and its feasibility reassessed.

3.6 Applications of symbolic execution

There are a number of uses for the output from symbolic execution. They
are: path domain checking, test data generation, assertion checking and
program reduction. Software maintenance can also benefit from symbolic
execution when inserting changes in a program and as an aid to regression
testing.

3.6.1 Path domain checking

When a path is executed with a single case it may result in:

- incorrect output due to one or more faults (universally incorrect);
- correct output although a fault exists (coincidentally correct);
- correct output and no faults exist (universally correct).

Distinguishing between a coincidentally correct output and a universally
correct output requires more than just execution of a path by a single case.
The output from a symbolic execution is more general as it represents
all the cases that could execute the path. Individual case values may be
substituted into the symbolic expression and evaluated by hand but this is
laborious.

It may be worthwhile for the tester to select cases from the test case
domain such that both minimum and maximum values for the variables
are used to evaluate the expression. For example, consider the following
variable declarations:

GrossPay	pic 9(4)
TaxFree	pic 9(4)
TaxPcent	pic 9(3)
NetPay	pic s9(4) sign leading separate.

Here *GrossPay*, *TaxFree* and *Percent* are input variables and *NetPay*
is output. In addition to the picture declaration *TaxPcent* is constrained
to the range 0 to 100. The program fragment introduced at the beginning
of this chapter is used to determine the value of *NetPay*. Minimum and
maximum values would be as follows:

Minimum	$GrossPay = 0000$	
	$TaxPcent = 000$	giving $NetPay = 0000$
	$TaxFree = 0000$	
Maximum	$GrossPay = 9999$	
	$TaxPcent = 100$	giving $NetPay = 9999$
	$TaxFree = 9999$	

Mixing minimum values for some variables with maximum values for other
variables may also prove valuable for example:

$$GrossPay = 0000$$
$$TaxPcent = 100 \qquad \text{giving } NetPay = -9999$$
$$TaxFree = 9999$$

This result appears to suggest a need for further constraints in the program such as:

$$GrossPay >= TaxFree$$

to only allow the creation of positive $NetPay$ values.

3.6.2 Test data generation

The expression produced for each output variable, when substituted with actual values in place of symbolic values, effectively becomes a test case. During the process of path domain checking, the task of selecting values in place of symbolic values is performed by hand. The tester's knowledge of possible problem cases (heuristics) may be used to create more stressful cases.

An alternative is that the process may be automated by using an optimizer. Here the path condition is used as a set of constraints. The objective function may be any expression containing the variables present in the path condition. One possible strategy produces many test cases for each path. The symbolic expression for each output variable on a path is then used in turn as an objective function. The optimizer is executed twice for each objective function, once to maximize it and once to minimize. This results in each path being executed twice as many times as there are output variables. For example, if a path is associated with three output variables, then six cases would be generated. Given that the functions are continuous this would be a useful set of cases, increasing confidence in the likely outputs of all intermediate values.

Where the constraints are not easily solved, techniques using random selection of values may be used [Ram76, Hed81]. When using random selection there is a practical need to set a range of values from which to select. Failure to set such a range results in large number solutions which cause overflow on execution. Unfortunately, setting upper and lower bounds may remove a solution from consideration. If no solution is found with the range imposed, then the bounds must be relaxed incrementally until a solution is discovered.

Hedley [Hed81] discovered that the only predicates remaining unsolved due to an imposed range on the values were those which contained numeric constants. Through experimentation he set out to determine the closest bounds that would generally produce solutions. He found these to be plus and minus twice the largest absolute value found in the predicates.

Partition analysis

Partition analysis is a technique that makes use of the output from symbolic execution to determine test data [Ric81]. It uses symbolic execution to identify sub-domains of the input data domain. Symbolic execution is performed on both the program and the specification. The resulting expressions are then used to produce sub-domains, such that each sub-domain is treated identically by both the program and the specification. Where a part of the input domain cannot be allocated to such a sub-domain, then either a structural or functional fault has been discovered in the program or the specification. In the system described by Richardson [Ric81] the specification is expressed in a manner close to program code. For this technique to prove practical, enhancements are required such that specifications can be expressed in a less program-like format.

3.6.3 Assertion checking

Assertions can range from a general, complex statement about, say, the contents of a table, to a simple statement about the value of a single variable. Simple assertions can be verified by symbolic execution, but more complex assertions cannot be easily accommodated.

A simple assertion may be placed on any branch in a program. It need not affect the normal execution of the program, but can be used during symbolic execution to assess the validity of the path. When symbolic execution along a path encounters an assertion it is treated in the same way as any other predicate. If its truth can be resolved, then symbolic execution either halts due to infeasibility in the case of false, or is discarded in the case of true. If its truth is unresolved, then it is conjoined to the path condition.

When the addition of assertions to a path condition turns a feasible path into an infeasible path, then the assertions have been violated. This indicates that an error is present in the path (or in the specification of the assertion).

The following straight-line form of a path contains assertions marked by 'a'. Suppose that an error is present indicated by 'e'.

1		move 0 to *total*
	e	move -1 to *counter*
2	a	$[total >= 0]$
	a	$[counter >= 0]$
		accept *score*
		move *continue* to *action*
3		$[score < 1]$
6		$[score <> 0]$
		move *stop* to *action*
15		$[action = stop]$

a	[*average* $<=$ *maxscore*]
a	[*average* $>=$ 0]
19	[*counter* $>$ 0]
	display 'No values have been input'
24	[*action* = stop]

Symbolic execution proceeds in the usual way. On reaching branch 2 the path condition is empty. The assertion *total* $>=$ 0 can instantly be verified as true because *total* has just been set to 0. Hence, the assertion need not be placed on the path condition. The assertion *counter* $>=$ 0 can also be verified, but in this case it is false: *counter* has previously been set to -1 in direct conflict with the assertion. Symbolic execution fails due to the failed assertion that arose because of the incorrect initialization of *counter*.

Assume, now, that a path is undergoing symbolic execution and is reaching the end of branch 16. The current expression for average is represented by:

$$(score_1 + score_2 + score_3)/3$$

where $score_n$ represents the nth value input to score.

The assertion *average* $<=$ *maxscore* is now substituted in the expressions for *average* and *maxscore* giving:

$$(score_1 + score_2 + score_3)/3 <= 7$$

The truth of this predicate cannot be evaluated so it is conjoined to the path condition. If there is a solution to the final path condition, then the assertion is upheld. If there is no solution to the final path condition, even though the path condition without the assertion is feasible, then the assertion fails. However, placing an assertion on a path that is infeasible determines nothing about the validity of the assertion.

3.6.4 Program reduction

King describes how symbolic execution can be used to achieve program reduction [Kin81]. This is the act of taking a program and producing another program containing fewer statements. The result is 'a simpler program consistent with the original but, operating over a smaller domain' [Kin81]. This is useful when reusing software where only a subset of the cases handled are required. A major step forward will have taken place in software engineering when the reuse of software is normal practice. Program reduction is a step towards this goal. This technique is not considered further in this book.

3.6.5 Software maintenance

Two problems facing the software maintainer are avoiding the introduction of unexecutable code and coping with the large volume of regression tests required.

In preparing program changes the maintainer often spends time on ascertaining the constraints which govern variables at the proposed points of insertion in the new code. This effort is required in order to avoid the introduction of unexecutable code. The converse of this situation also arises: unexecutable code is introduced because the maintainer is unaware of the prevailing constraints.

Symbolic execution can be used to reduce the likelihood of introducing unexecutable code, to speed up the process of determining the constraints on variables at a given point in a program and to reduce the volume of regression testing.

Modifications

When modifying software the impact of a change can be categorised as either a domain change or a computation change. A **domain change** is caused by introducing a new selection statement or by changing an existing one. This creates new paths or changes the range of values that can execute some existing paths. A **computation change** affects the outputs that result from executing a path. Computation changes often cause a different path to be followed for a given input case, but these can be regarded as side-effects rather than as primary changes. In many instances new computations are introduced for specific domains. Ensuring that the intended domain, and only the intended domain, is affected by a new computation is a major part of the maintenance activity.

The areas of concern when modifying software can be classified as follows:

- Are the given domains processed by the new code?
- Are all other domains not processed by the new code?
- Has the introduction of a selection statement introduced a new domain or has an unnecessary selection statement been introduced?

A Class 1 error occurs when only a subset of the intended domain is processed by the newly inserted code. Suppose some process, X, is to be undertaken for values of A in the range 10-19 inclusive. In the following program fragment, lines 15-18 have been inserted with this intention.

```
01    A pic 99

        ⋮

10    if A > 10
11    then

        ⋮
```

```
15        if A < 20
16        then
17             do X
18        end-if
          ⋮
31   end-if
```

At line 11 A can take a value in the range 11-99 inclusive. At line 15 the range of values of A is reduced to 11-19 inclusive. As a result, $A = 10$ is not included in the domain being subjected to process X.

A Class 2 error occurs when a superset of the intended domain is processed by the newly inserted code. Consider again the process X which is again to be undertaken for values of A in the range 10-19 inclusive. In the following different program fragment, lines 15-18 have been inserted with this intention.

```
01   A pic 99
     ⋮
10   if A > 9
11   then

          ⋮
15        if A < 21
16        then
17             do X
18        end-if
          ⋮
31   end-if
```

At line 11 A can take a value in the range 10-99 inclusive. At line 15 the range of values of A is reduced to 10-20 inclusive. As a result the domain $A = 10$-19 is subjected to process X but, in addition, $A = 20$ is also subjected to X.

Class 3 errors occur when a selection statement includes values that are excluded by previous selection statements; thus creating branches that cannot be executed. For example consider the following program fragment:

```
10   if A > 10
11   then

          ⋮
20        if A < 50
21        then

               ⋮
25             if A > 75
26             then
```

⋮   ⋮
29   end-if

⋮

31   end-if
32   end-if

At line 21 the range of values that A could take is 11-49. The introduction of lines 25, 26,.. is superfluous because A must be less than 50 to reach this point, the additional condition of $A > 75$ has already been guaranteed to be false.

Class 4 errors occur when the truth of the condition in a selection statement has already been established by earlier selection statements. Consider again the example used above for discussing class 3 errors, except that line 25 is changed to $A < 75$. The selection at line 20 has guaranteed that $A < 50$ is true, so the test of $A < 75$ is superfluous as it will always be true.

Impact of module hierarchy on path infeasibility

Avoiding infeasible paths during software maintenance is a difficulty compounded by the impact of modules higher up the calling hierarchy. These superordinate modules determine the domains of the input parameters, and so are integral to the problem of infeasible paths. When a conditional statement is inserted such that no feasible path is found for its branches, the conditional predicates that contribute to the infeasibility may be found locally either in the calling module or in a module higher up the calling hierarchy.

When faced with changing one module out of a large system of modules the maintainer faces an escalated form of the infeasible path problem. It is not sufficient to be able to place the modification on a path assessed as feasible in the module if the constraints placed on that module by the calling modules are such that the new code cannot be executed. What is required is a means of assessing feasibility–both locally and for the wider chain of module invocations.

Regression testing

To avoid unintentional changes to existing parts of a program going unnoticed a rigorous testing phase is often undertaken. This is known as **regression testing**. Here, a set of test cases are executed and the results compared to the results obtained from the same test cases run through the unmodified version of a system. If the new version has remained unaltered for these functions, then the results for these cases from both versions of the program will match. Any differences indicate an unexpected change.

A large set of test cases may have been used to test the software when it was first developed. It is useful to identify a subset of these tests for regression testing. Work on selection of test cases for revalidation has been undertaken by Fischer [Fis77]; Yau and Kashimoto [Yau87]; and Hartman and Robson [Har90].

Yau and Kashimoto's approach involves constructing a cause-effect graph for the newly constructed program and then dividing the program's input domain into several classes. These classes are used to generate test cases. After the program has been modified the input partitions are derived again, and the original set of test cases searched for a subset of cases which provide coverage of each of the new partitions. Those partitions which cannot be covered require the generation of new cases. Both these new cases and the sub-set of the original cases are then executed with parallel symbolic execution. Symbolic execution is undertaken to provide debugging information.

This approach is reported to be successful with programs that undertake classification of input, such as determining whether three integers represent either an equilateral or isosceles or a scalene triangle, but is less successful for algorithmic programs such as sorting.

Fischer proposed the use of a 0-1 integer programming technique to determine the test cases to be used for regression testing. A program is parsed and represented as three matrices: connectivity; reachability; and variable set/use. The first two represent the control flow of the program and the third contains details of the dataflow. A fourth matrix, the test case dependency matrix, records the coverage of each test case. The objective of the approach is to determine the minimum number of test cases to provide coverage of the program.

Hartmann and Robson have attempted to extend Fischer's method by including parameter information in the set/use matrix. They also have announced their intention to apply it to several languages and to develop tools to automate test case selection.

Fisher's approach, including the extensions proposed by Hartmann and Robson, presumes that the execution of a branch just once provides an adequate test. Unfortunately, adoption of this technique will not overcome the problem of coincidental correctness: a test case may yield the correct output for a case where another case, causing execution of the same path, would yield an erroneous result. To guard against the problem of coincidental correctness multiple path executions are necessary, but, unfortunately, are still not sufficient.

Avoiding infeasible modifications using symbolic execution

The practice of treating module calls as an I/O boundary in symbolic execution is not helpful when infeasiblity is caused by conflicting constraints that are in different modules. Adoption of the macro-expansion approach to symbolic execution overcomes this problem. Unfortunately, this approach could suffer from the path explosion problem, where there are many paths available. However, judicious use of a path selection strategy such as coverage of a branch at least once avoids this problem, and symbolic execution provides a useful means of assessing all three maintenance problems which are caused by domain and computation errors.

Errors where either a subset or superset of the correct domain is processed are easily detected. Test cases can be generated at the minimum and maximum values for the variables in the newly inserted conditional statements. If these do not cater for the extremes of the domains to be covered, or include values not intended, then a domain error is identified–even without executing the generated test case.

Situations where the introduction of a particular conditional statement would be superfluous can also be identified using symbolic execution. An assertion postulating the opposite of the intended condition is inserted at the point under consideration for the conditional statement; for example, in the program fragment describing class 3 modifications errors shown on page 57, the assertion would be $A <= 75$. If this assertion is not upheld, then there is no need for the conditional statement on this path. However, the number of paths to be investigated before the conditional statement can confidently be dropped should not be underestimated.

Regression testing using symbolic execution

Rather than execute all the original test cases, the set of paths covered by these tests should be established. The result is a set of critical regression testing paths. Each of these critical paths can then be symbolically executed (just once) for both the old and new versions of the program.

For each path, the path condition is compared between the two versions and the output expressions for each variable are also compared. When the path conditions do not match, a domain error has been detected. When the path conditions match, but one or more of the variable expressions do not, then a computation error has been identified. This technique is capable of replacing many conventional test executions by just one symbolic execution.

CHAPTER 4

Existing symbolic execution systems

The antecedent of many symbolic execution systems is EXDAMS [Bal69]. This was a monitoring system constructed before the first symbolic execution which required the program being tested to be executed with data values. While the program executes it is closely monitored and a history of the execution is stored. It provides a flexible approach to the examination of such a history. An analysis of the source program is undertaken to provide a data table and model of the program. These are used in conjunction with the history to provide the user with a view of the program's state at any point during the execution.

After EXDAMS, many software testing and debugging tools made use of symbolic execution. Some of these systems incorporate features similar to those provided by EXDAMS. There are now thirteen systems whose authors claim make use of symbolic execution. These are EFFIGY [Kin75, Kin76], SELECT [Boy75], ATTEST [Cla76a,Cla76b], CASEGEN [Ram76], DISSECT [How77, How78a], EL1 [Che79,Plo79], SMOTL [Bic79], Interactive Programming System (IPS) [Asi79], SADAT [Vog80], the FORTRAN testbed [Hed81], IVTS [Tay83], UNISEX [Kem85] and SYMBAD [Coe90]. The languages processed by these systems are mainly confined to relatively mature, third-generation, procedural languages, although one or two process non-procedural languages such as LISP; in the case of these latter languages the principles involved are the same.

Additionally, MALPAS [Web87, One88] and SPADE [Car86,One89] are two commercially available systems for which there are no detailed descriptions in the academic literature. The few papers that do describe the systems outline the facilities provided, but give no description of their inner mechanisms. However, both MALPAS and SPADE appear to make use of symbolic execution.

The nature of the symbolic execution utilized in the fifteen systems varies from one system to the next.

4.1 Minimum features of a symbolic execution testing system

The minimum features that a system should exhibit before it can be considered to make use of symbolic execution are:

- it produces a path condition for each path examined;
- it determines whether a path condition is feasible;
- for each output variable it produces a symbolic expression in terms of input variables and constants.

Using these three features as criteria for rejection causes EXDAMS, DISSECT, EL1 symbolic executor, SMOTL, SADAT, IVTS and UNISEX to be removed from the list of symbolic execution systems.

EXDAMS has never been claimed as a symbolic execution system. Paths are executed with actual data and no symbolic expressions are maintained. Hence, no feasibility checking can be undertaken.

The DISSECT system produces expressions for variables and a path condition for each path specified. It fails to check the consistency of the predicates of the path condition; this task is left for the user to undertake by hand.

The EL1 symbolic evaluator does not create symbolic expressions for output variables nor does it determine path feasibility. SMOTL does not create expressions for variables, nor maintain a path condition. Its path analysis is based on maintaining maximum and minimum values for each variable. It uses these values to check for predicate contradiction and hence path feasibility. This is not symbolic execution but, nevertheless, it achieves one of the results that can be produced by symbolic execution: the generation of test cases for a path. Other results achieved using symbolic execution, such as assertion checking, are derived from the expressions maintained for the path condition and each variable. SMOTL cannot achieve these results because the expressions are not maintained by the system. However, SMOTL does have a strategy for combining paths in an attempt to reduce the number required to cover all branches. This technique is applicable in all path based testing systems–including those using symbolic execution.

SADAT does not attempt to determine path feasibility: it leaves this for the user to perform by hand. Expressions are not determined for output variables. IVTS is still under development and it is the symbolic executor component of this system which is incomplete. As yet, the system does not determine path feasibility.

UNISEX is intended to be used as an expression simplifier and a theorem prover to assess path feasibility. In some cases the expression simplifier can resolve a path condition to either true or false. When this cannot be achieved the resulting expression will be passed to the theorem prover. The theorem prover has not yet been built. Currently the path condition is output for the user to assess by hand.

MALPAS and SPADE are two commercially available validation systems which stem from work sponsored by the Ministry of Defence. The systems appear to share some features which is a result of their common origin. There are a few papers in the literature describing these systems [Car86,

Web87, One88, One89], but there are no published papers describing their inner mechanisms and the problems encountered in their development. In addition to the summary papers, publicity material is readily available. The following descriptions are based on both of these sources.

MALPAS (MALvern Program Analysis Suite) transforms the source program into an intermediate form and determines the number of paths through the program. A static analysis is undertaken to spot anomalies such as two writes without an intervening assignment. Also, the input variables which determine the value of each output variable on each path are identified, together with a list of the predicates at each node which must hold for a path to be executed.

Finally, the system determines which of the paths are feasible and which are infeasible. No description is given of how this is achieved but, given the data that is maintained to this point, it looks likely that some form of symbolic execution is undertaken together with feasibility checking of the resultant path condition. Results are displayed for each path in the following form:

if path condition
then
$\quad$ $var_1 = Expr_1$
$\quad$ $\vdots$
$\quad$ $var_n = Expr_n$
end-if

Assertions may be inserted into the source program which are checked against the path condition. This cannot always be achieved; in such a case, the expression is output for the programmer to inspect. It is not stated how this assessment is made, nor under what circumstances the assessment cannot be made.

SPADE (Southampton Program Analysis and Development Environment) produces an intermediate form known as FDL (Functional Description Language). At present translators exist for Pascal and INTEL-8080, with translators for Ada and Modula-2 being planned. A part of the system known as the FDL Reader assesses the intermediate form for syntactic errors. This seems to be unnecessary as this duplicates processing undertaken by the language compiler. However, users can write FDL directly as a specification and the FDL Reader is then used as the only syntax checker. Anomalies such as unreachable code and unused variables are identified as well as an analysis of module interfaces.

It is not clear from the published material how paths are selected, but path conditions are established. Symbolic execution of a path is undertaken and the output is claimed to be 'useful' for test data selection, but it does not generate specific test cases. No details are given about the assessment of path infeasibility.

The proof checker is used as a documentation tool for proving the program. It contains tools for arithmetic and logical expression simplification together with limited automatic deduction facilities. A data base of rules is maintained. The user guides the checker in search of a proof.

By excluding the systems which do not exhibit the three crucial criteria and those systems for which there is little detailed material in the literature, there remain seven systems: EFFIGY, SELECT, ATTEST, CASEGEN, IPS, the FORTRAN testbed and SYMBAD. These systems can be considered true symbolic execution testing systems.

4.2 Strengths and weaknesses of current systems

The strengths that should be incorporated into future symbolic execution systems and the weaknesses and omissions of each of the seven identified systems are outlined.

4.2.1 EFFIGY – An interactive symbolic execution system

EFFIGY was the first system to make use of symbolic execution. It was designed to allow a program to be developed and tested gradually, making use of the symbolic execution facility as well as execution with actual data values. It is a development tool which can be used when testing either program fragments as they are written or complete programs.

The interactive nature of the system is one of its strengths, since it allows a degree of flexibility: when a path is being evaluated the user may insert actual values as well as symbolic values. This results in expressions for some variables containing a mixture of symbolic and actual values. A symbolic trace of a path can be obtained. This shows the state of specified variables line by line.

A powerful feature of EFFIGY is the use of assert statements which can be verified. These are based upon the symbolic representations of the variables and the path condition.

Perhaps the most important omission from the EFFIGY system, given that it is interactive, is the absence of a facility to provide a view of the flowgraph or a coverage metric. It is possible that a user could terminate a session with EFFIGY having discovered many faults, corrected them, been satisfied with the modifications but then have omitted some branches of the program. It would be helpful if an indication of the extent to which the analysis has covered the flowgraph was provided. No long term recording of coverage statistics appears to be maintained; although it is stated that an exhaustive 'test manager', for which no details are given, is a part of the system.

No strategy for path selection is incorporated into the system. The users must employ their own testing heuristics to create a strategy. The selection of the appropriate branch, when this is not determined by the state of the path condition, is left for the user; so too is any decision on the number of iterations to be made at each loop. Determining the feasibility of paths is achieved using a theorem prover.

There is no direct reference in the literature to how EFFIGY handles module calls. However, Hantler and King [Han76] describe the lemma approach. Both of them worked on the construction of EFFIGY and it is likely that this is the method used in EFFIGY.

Perhaps EFFIGY's major weakness is that it handles only a small subset of the language being analysed. The main weaknesses of EFFIGY can be summarized as:

- only a subset of the processed language can be used;
- there is no strategy for path selection;
- there is no output of coverage metrics.

4.2.2 SELECT

SELECT [Boy75] (Symbolic Execution Language to Enable Comprehensive Testing) was constructed at about the same time as the EFFIGY system. It attempts to provide similar facilities to EFFIGY and, in addition, creates values which can act as test cases. These values are generated as a by-product of evaluating path conditions. The system was built to process programs written in a subset of LISP. It is not clear what class of application the system is aimed at.

SELECT produces 3 categories of output for each processed path:

- test data;
- simplified symbolic expressions for each program variable on a path;
- statements of correctness of user supplied assertions.

SELECT also identifies some infeasible program paths.

The system aims to be automatic and is claimed to have a path selection strategy where the aim is coverage of every branch. Paths are created by commencing at the start of the program and adding one branch at a time until a halt is reached. Each time a branch is added to the path condition it is passed to an inequality solver to determine path feasibility. Both linear and non-linear inequality solvers are employed. The solver maximizes an arbitrary objective function and the solution to the path condition of the whole path is used as a test case.

SELECT requires that, for loops which may be executed a variable number of times, the user specifies the number of iterations to be included in the path. The system updates the path condition and variable expressions for each iteration of the loop.

Subroutines are tested in isolation until they are deemed satisfactory. Whenever a subroutine is invoked, the set of path conditions for that routine may be incorporated into the path which invokes it. This adds to the combinatorial explosion of the number of possible paths. Boyer suggests that a better approach might be to make use of input and output assertions for each subroutine [Boy75]. This would not increase the number of paths.

The ambiguous array reference problem, where arrays are indexed by input variables, is tackled by the introduction of virtual paths. This adds to the complexity of the flowgraph by adding a branch for each element of the array. The weaknesses of SELECT can be summarized as:

- only a subset of LISP can be processed;

- its approach to ambiguous array elements increases the number of paths;

- its use of macro-expansion increases the number of paths.

4.2.3 ATTEST

The prime objective of ATTEST is to generate test data for a path [Cla76b, Cla76a]. This is done using the conditions and assignments of the path to ensure that the data will force execution of that path. A secondary output, produced almost as a by-product, is a symbolic representation of the output variables of the path in terms of the input variables and constants. The system will sometimes inform the user if the path is infeasible and cannot therefore be executed because no such data set exists. The system cannot detect all infeasible paths. In particular, it cannot identify infeasibility where the system of constraints is non-linear. This is surprising: one would expect FORTRAN programs to contain non-linear predicates.

ATTEST's main strength is significant. It analyzes FORTRAN programs and, hence, was a step towards a widely usable symbolic execution testing system which can be used in either automatic or interactive mode.

The difficult task of selecting the paths for analysis is not tackled by the system, but left entirely to the user. Paths for analysis can be specified in two ways: statically or interactively. The static specification requires the whole path to be specified at once, while the interactive mode allows the user to select one branch at a time as each conditional statement is reached.

When a constraint makes the path infeasible the user is informed and the analysis proceeds to the next path. When the end of a path is reached, and it is feasible, then the final solution obtained is a test case that will cause execution of the path.

The system attempts to discover where array indices stray out of bounds using two temporary constraints. One specifies that the upper bound must not be exceeded and the other that the lower bound must not be achieved. For example, consider an array $A(5..10)$. Constraints of *index* < 5 and *index* > 10 are used. When either of these temporary constraints is conjoined to the path condition the constraint should prove contradictory if the path will not allow the index to stray out of bounds. When ambiguous array elements are encountered the symbolic execution halts.

No path selection is undertaken by the system. The user must input the paths which are to be evaluated. When path constraints are checked for feasibility they are passed only to a linear inequality solver. However, the system analyses FORTRAN programs which might be expected to contain non-linear constraints.

The processing of module calls uses macro-expansion. This does not cause a path explosion problem for the system because no recording of path coverage appears to be undertaken. It merely increases the length of the path. There is also no facility for insertion and verification of assertions.

The weaknesses of ATTEST can be summarized as:

- it cannot detect infeasibility of all paths;
- it carries out no path selection;
- symbolic execution halts on encountering ambiguous array elements;
- there is no recording of test coverage;
- there is no facility for assertion checking.

4.2.4 CASEGEN

CASEGEN generates test data and, like ATTEST, analyses FORTRAN programs [Ram76]. The system operates entirely in batch mode and consists of four components:

- a FORTRAN source code processor;
- a path generator;
- a path constraint generator;
- a test data generator.

The FORTRAN source code processor analyses the program code and generates a data base consisting of a flowgraph, a symbol table and an internal representation of the source code. The path generator uses the database to produce a set of paths to cover all branches. The authors do not discuss the path selection strategy, except to state that loops are executed a fixed number of times. For each path the path constraint generator produces the path condition. However, some of the paths generated may be infeasible.

The test data generator aims to create values for the input variables that satisfy the set of inequalities for each path, hence creating a test case for each path. The sets of inequalities in the path condition are solved using linear programming, integer programming, mixed programming and non-linear programming techniques as appropriate. A procedure based on systematic trial and error and random number generation is also used. This use of several types of optimizer makes this system superior to ATTEST in terms of feasibility checking. Nevertheless, it is error-prone, for example in one publication the numbers (26,7,7) were generated for the sides of an isosceles triangle [Ram76].

The builders of CASEGEN acknowledge the difficult aspects of symbolic execution. For example, ambiguous array reference is retained during symbolic execution and is resolved during test data generation. While the builders acknowledge the difficulties of handling module calls, they do not make clear what approach has been adopted in CASEGEN. Output of the variable expressions and path condition are not provided and there are no facilities for insertion and evaluation of assertions.

The weaknesses of CASEGEN can be summarized as:

- it does not provide an output of a path condition;
- there is no output of expressions for variables;
- it does not process assertions.

4.2.5 IPS

IPS [Asi79] is a collection of integrated software support tools for the design, development and maintenance of large computer programs. It was built as a general software development tool for a language available on a small computer: MINIPL/1. There is no statement in the literature concerning the success of the system in the field but it was built in conjunction with Olivetti and was destined for commercial use.

The interactive part of the system is mainly concerned with symbolic execution. Its strengths centre around the state recording and review facilities. Whenever a conditional statement is encountered the user is required to select the branch to be pursued. The state of the path condition and variables at each conditional statement are recorded. The user may return to any previously encountered conditional statement and examine the states of the path condition and variables.

Assertions may be introduced into the program. The system will determine the consistency between the assertion and the path condition. The flexibility provided by the interactive nature of the system is used to overcome the absence of a path selection strategy. While arrays and calls are handled the mechanisms employed are not made clear.

The weaknesses of IPS can be summarized as:

- only a small subset of a little known programming language is processed;
- there are no path selection facilities.

4.2.6 FORTRAN test bed

This tool [Hed81, Hen83] undertakes static and dynamic analysis of FOR-TRAN programs and the construction of paths. It also generates test cases which will cause the execution of the paths. It is the path construction and test case generation that are of concern here as they make use of symbolic execution.

The tool is centred around the concept of an LCSAJ [Hen76]. An LCSAJ (linear code sequence and jump) is a series of statements ending with a transfer of control out of a linear code sequence. Paths can be viewed as a series of LCSAJs. Determining whether each LCSAJ is feasible can be the first step in determining feasibility of a path. Should a single LCSAJ be infeasible, then any path which contains it is infeasible. A path whose LCSAJs are all feasible, is not necessarily feasible. Two LCSAJs together may give rise to infeasibility. In this system LCSAJs are gradually added together until either the addition of an LCSAJ results in the creation of an infeasible path, or the path is complete and feasible. The path selection strategy does not deal with loop iterations, but leaves this for the user to specify.

The FORTRAN test-bed determines the feasibility of an LCSAJ or a series of LCSAJs by employing symbolic execution. The system will solve sets of linear inequalities provided by the path condition to produce test data. The system makes use of random number generation to solve non-linear inequalities. This approach is similar to that employed by CASEGEN. The FORTRAN test-bed has an additional feature which makes use of a function to establish bounds for the random number generation. It is based on the constants in the inequalities. In a series of tests the system solved and generated test data for paths that covered all but 2.7% of LCSAJs.

Most module calls are handled by macro-expansion. This increases the number of paths available for consideration. Functions, however, are treated as input statements and new symbolic values are provided. It is not clear why different strategies are employed for function calls and other calls because treating both as I/O interfaces would maintain the boundary identified during design.

The system analyses FORTRAN programs and, with a few minor exceptions, this is ANSI standard FORTRAN. It is worth stressing that symbolic execution is used as just one technique employed by a software testing system that provides a variety of testing facilities ranging from static analysis to test case generation. The test bed is a commercially used system and cannot be regarded as just a researcher's experimental system.

The main weakness of the FORTRAN testbed is that it does not process assertions.

4.2.7 SYMBAD

SYMBAD (SYMBolic executor of sequential ADA programs) is one of the most recently developed systems [Coe90]. It processes Ada units with the exception of those that contain tasks: the mechanism used in Ada for defining parallel processes.

The first stage employed by SYMBAD is translation into an intermediate form which is common LISP. The next stage is a combined path selection and symbolic execution process. When a branch point in the program is encountered the current path condition is examined by a theorem prover to determine whether the encountered branch condition is true, false or undetermined. If the condition is true or false, then symbolic execution continues down the relevant selected branch. When undetermined the user selects the branch to be followed and the appropriate condition is conjoined to the path condition. Symbolic execution then continues down the chosen branch.

Assertions are checked by the system. They are embedded within the source code as comments and are checked against the path condition when they are encountered during the symbolic execution.

The authors claim to have incorporated a new method of processing arrays which overcomes the difficulty of ambiguous array references. An array is represented by an ordered set of pairs, where each pair contains details of an assignment encountered on the path. The first item in the pair is the value of the index, the second is the value assigned to that element. Consider the variable A declared as:

A : array($1 \ldots max$) of integer

and the following program fragment:

```
8    get(J);
9    A(J) := 5;
10   A(J + 1) := 7;
11   if A(4) > 1
         ⋮
```

When variable A is declared it is given the pair:

$$A : (any, undef)$$

indicating that all elements of the array are undefined. At line 8 J is arbitrarily assigned a symbolic value:

$$J : J@1$$

At line 9 'A' has a second pair added to its set:

$$A : (any, undef)(J@1, 5)$$

and after line 10 a third pair is added:

$$A : (any, undef)(J@1, 5)(J@1 + 1, 7)$$

Line 11 is unresolved because the value of $J@1$ is symbolic, so the user must choose a branch–say the true branch. The predicate must now be placed on the path condition. By searching the set of pairs belonging to A it can be seen that one of the following must be true for $A(4) > 1$ to be true:

$$J@1 = 4 \qquad J@1 + 1 = 4$$

The path condition cannot sensibly contain both of these predicates as they are in direct contradiction so one must be chosen, but which one? This is not discussed by the authors, which is unfortunate because this is the heart of the array problem. Eventually, a choice must be made and this means selecting an actual value.

This method appears to be similar to earlier ones which deferred resolution of ambiguous array references until test data generation. In those early systems paths were not assessed for feasibility, so this posed no problem. Here, path feasibility is assessed, so a decision must be made. The method does have the benefit of maintaining information until a branch point which requires the resolution of the ambiguity is reached. However, experience suggests that such branches follow closely after the occurrence of the ambiguous array reference so there may be only a small benefit to be gained from maintaining the ordered set of pairs.

No description is given of how module calls are processed. The system does not generate test cases. The path condition is output and the user must solve this by hand to create an appropriate test case for the path. The weakness of SYMBAD is that test cases are not generated.

4.3 The ideal symbolic execution testing system

The notion of an ideal system ignores the practical considerations of construction. A system that delivers the features of an ideal system but which, for example, takes a long time to process, is clearly not ideal. Requirements of an ideal system are likely to be contradictory and a practical system must be a compromise between the conflicting requirements. Nevertheless, it is useful to set out an optimist's system against which existing and potential systems may be compared.

4.3.1 Input

The primary input to such a system is the source program which may contain assertions. Further inputs will be required in response to the results obtained:

- a specification of paths to be evaluated;
- changes to assertions;
- a simple mechanism for the input of the expected results for generated test data either as a range of values or a single value.

4.3.2 Output

The power of a symbolic execution testing system is determined by the variety and utility of the information provided. This should include:

- diagrammatic representation of the program flow-graph;
- paths (lists of constituent statements);
- the path condition and an indication of feasibility or the constraint which turns the path infeasible;
- expressions for output and intermediate variables;
- statements which report the on truth of each assertion;
- test data;
- results of execution;
- comparison of results with expectation;
- statements which describe the coverage obtained in the testing already undertaken.

The utility of the output may be enhanced by providing a variety of viewing facilities:

- a display of specified variables or the path condition in specified paths at specified points;
- a trace through the symbolic execution of a path at various speeds;
- a trace through the execution of user provided test cases;
- a trace which describes both symbolic and test case execution simultaneously;
- a coverage report at any point in the testing process

4.3.3 Path selection

Current methods of path selection employ only simple strategies such as: take the left branch first, generate the shortest path. These strategies have a common target: that of achieving a particular coverage metric such as all statements or all branches or all LCSAJs are executed at least once. Each of these strategies is prone to the problem of selecting infeasible paths. Having identified a set of paths which cover, say, all branches, some of the selected paths will be found to be infeasible. This leaves the problem of identifying feasible paths which includes the non-covered branches from the infeasible paths. This strategy does not consider the effectiveness of the paths selected and whether the paths are, in some way, more useful or interesting than other paths.

An alternative approach may be to attempt to identify paths and associated test cases that are, in some way, representative of a large set of cases. The ideal symbolic execution testing system should incorporate a path selection strategy in which the expressions produced by the symbolic execution are utilised in an attempt to identify 'interesting' paths.

The ideal system also requires novel solutions to the problems presented by loops, arrays and module calls.

4.3.4 A multi-language symbolic execution system

Researchers have reflected on the possibility of producing a general symbolic execution testing system which may be used regardless of the language in which the source program is written. Such a system should exhibit two necessary features. First, there is a need for a translator from each source language into the single intermediate representation processed by the evaluator. The intermediate representation must, therefore, cater for all features of the set of source languages. Second, output messages from the execution system should be meaningful to the user. For example, when path infeasibility has been detected by the system the output should clearly identify the path and the predicate which made the path condition infeasible. The most instructive format for this output is where it refers to the source program submitted to the system. To achieve this requires the maintenance of references to the original source program.

An alternative attainable target may be a symbolic execution testing system that analyses programs written in a widely used language. For example, until SYM-BOL,no symbolic execution system has been built for a commercial data processing language such as COBOL. Whatever the language, it should also handle the main features of that language. Adherence to a widely adopted standard, such as an ANSI standard, would be beneficial.

4.4 Ideal, existing and new symbolic execution systems

Tables 4.1, 4.2, 4.3 and 4.3 summarize the features of a number of systems. The first system to be built that satisfied the minimum criteria for a symbolic execution system was EFFIGY. It is also EFFIGY that appears closest to the ideal system. All subsequent systems were, in some senses, a step backwards from the standard set by EFFIGY.

The only major weaknesses of EFFIGY when compared to later systems are its failure to adopt a widespread language and its inability to devise test cases to satisfy a path condition. The authors do not state the language

Table 4.1 *Symbolic execution systems compared I.*

System	Language analysed	Input	Output
EFFIGY	Simple PL/1	Source program assertions	Symbolic values, truth of assertions
IPS	PL/1 subset	Source program assertions	Symbolic expressions Path condition, truth assertions
FORTRAN testbed	FORTRAN	Source program paths	Test cases infeasible paths
SYMBAD	Ada sequential units only	Source program assertions	Symbolic expressions, path condition, state of assertions
SYM-BOL	Large COBOL subset	Source program assertions	Path, path condition variable expressions, truth of coverage test, test cases
SELECT	LISP subset	Source program assertions	Not stated
CASEGEN	FORTRAN	Source program	Paths, test cases
ATTEST	FORTRAN	Source program	Symbolic expressions, test cases
SMOTL	SMOD	Source program	Minimal set of test cases giving branch coverage
DISSECT	FORTRAN	Source program, DISSECT commands	Path in straight line form, path condition variable expressions, anomalies
SADAT	FORTRAN	Source program, SADAT commands	Path conditions for set of paths to cover all branches
IVTS	HAL/S	Source program	Anomalies, path condition
UNISEX	Large Pascal subset	Source program containing assertions	Reformatted source, path, path condition, truth of assertions
EL1	EL1 subset	Source program	Intermediate representation

Table 4.2 *Symbolic execution systems compared II.*

System	Automatic or interactive	Path selection	Path feasibility	Assertion testing
EFFIGY	Interactive	User selected	Every branch, theorem prover	Yes
IPS	Interactive	User control	Every branch, theorem prover	Yes
FORTRAN testbed	Automatic	Not stated	Every branch, algebraic linear and random	No
SYMBAD	Interactive	User selected	Every branch, theorem prover, linear	Yes
SYM-BOL	Automatic and interactive	User or automatic. Uses symbolic expressions to aid in selection	Every branch, algebraic linear, detects non-linear	Yes
SELECT	Automatic	All paths	Every branch, algebraic linear and non-linear	Yes
CASEGEN	Automatic	Minimal set cover all branches	Every branch algebraic linear, non-linear and random	No
ATTEST	Automatic and interactive	None	Every branch, agebraic only linear	No
SMOTL	Automatic	Connection of sub-paths, reduction strategy	Assesed from min. and max. values of variables	No
DISSECT	Batch	User selects	User by hand	No
SADAT	Batch	User selects	User by hand	No
IVTS	Interactive	User selects	User by hand	Yes
UNISEX	Automatic and interactive	True branch first	User by hand	Yes
EL1	Automatic	Unknown	Not undertaken	No

Table 4.3 *Symbolic execution systems compared III.*

System	Automatic/	Path selection	Psth feasibility	Assertion testing
EFFIGY	Interactive	User selected	Every branch	Yes
SELECT	Automatic	All paths	Every branch, Algebraic linear and non-linear	Yes
CASEGEN	Automatic	Minimal set cover all branches	Every branch, algebraic linear and non-linear random	No
ATTEST	Automatic and interactive	None	Every branch, algebraic only linear	No
IPS	Interactive	User control	When requested by user, theorem prover	Yes
FORTRAN testbed	Automatic	Not stated	Every branch, algebraic linear and random	No
SYMBAD	Interactive	User selected	Every branch, linear and random	Yes

Table 4.4 *Symbolic execution systems compared IV.*

System	Call handling	Loop handling	Arrays	Files	Strings
EFFIGY	I/O boundary	User selects	1-dim	No	No
SELECT	Macro expansion	User states maximum no. of iterations	Yes	No	No
CASEGEN	Not stated	Fixed number	Yes	No	No
ATTEST	Macro expansion	Fixed max. no. of iterations	Only constant indexes	No	No
IPS	Not stated	User selects	Not known	No	No
FORTRAN testbed	Macro expansion functions as I/O boundary	User specifies number of iterations	Maintains symbolic expressions	No	No
SYMBAD	Not stated	User selects	Yes	No	No

in which it is written but more important is the fact that it handles only a simple subset of PL/1. If the other systems were assessed in terms of their ability to handle similarly simple language subsets, then there is a possibility that they may appear at least as impressive as EFFIGY.

In a bid to make them more useful many of the subsequent systems handle larger language subsets and more popular languages. This has been achieved at the expense of a reduction in the capabilities of the systems. The two systems that are closest to EFFIGY in capability which handle an almost complete and popular language are the FORTRAN testbed and SYMBAD. If the FORTRAN testbed were to incorporate a mechanism for the specification of assertions then this would become closer to the ideal system than EFFIGY. SYMBAD and EFFIGY both require a means of generating test cases to satisfy the path condition in order to improve upon the FORTRAN test-bed.

Assertions could of course be written as normal source code. This would mean that following testing the program would be in need of modification to remove them. However, it could be argued that permanent assertions with appropriate error messages could provide a powerful run-time semantic monitor.

The notion of the 'best' symbolic execution system is a useful one. It may be used as the benchmark when assessing new systems. Unfortunately, it is difficult to determine which is the most useful system as there is no clearly outstanding system. EFFIGY perhaps comes the closest, but a few additional features would be required to provide a useful benchmark.

If a new system provides the features provided by EFFIGY and processes a commonly used language and generates test cases, then it would be a significant advance. The minimum features necessary to be comparable with this 'EFFIGY-plus' system are:

- input of source code containing assertions;
- interactive selection of paths;
- the output of symbolic values;
- the output of the truth or otherwise of assertions;
- the display of statements about path feasibility;
- the display of test cases.

Additional features necessary to justify the creation of a new system would be: the use of a widely employed language for a class of programs not currently accommodated and a path selection strategy for automatic systems. It is the development of a path selection strategy that is fundamental to the advancement of all forms of path-based testing, including the use of symbolic execution. Any tool that helps the user in selecting paths, or includes an improved strategy for automatic path selection, will be a contribution to research in path-based testing.

4.5 Weaknesses of symbolic execution

This section has two purposes. First, it summarizes the weaknesses described in the earlier chapters concerning the use of symbolic execution as a testing technique and the weaknesses of the tools that have been constructed to support its application. Second, it establishes a set of research aims whose solution is described in the following chapters.

4.5.1 Weaknesses in existing research

The weaknesses of existing research may be divided into two categories. The first category are the general problems identified for symbolic execution. The second category are the weaknesses of the tools built to support symbolic execution.

General problems of symbolic execution

There are four problem areas which are well documented in the literature concerning the application of symbolic execution. These are: path selection and the evaluation of loops; a dilemma over how to process module calls; the evaluation of array references dependent on input values and the checking of path feasibility.

There are three further problems concerning the application of numerical optimizers for checking feasibility which are not documented in the literature. These are: formulating predicates of the form $a \neq b$ as a constraint; passing strings to an optimizer; and recognizing conflicting constraints when constraints contain both records and fields within records.

Current methods of path selection employ only simple strategies such as take the true branch first or generate the shortest path. These strategies have a common target: that of achieving a particular coverage metric such as all statements or all branches are executed at least once. Each of these strategies is prone to the problem of selecting infeasible paths. Having identified a set of paths which cover, say all branches, some of the selected paths will be found to be infeasible. This leaves the problem of identifying feasible paths which include the non-covered branches from the infeasible paths.

Some systems that use symbolic execution have two distinct stages. First, select a path. Second, symbolically execute the selected path. Ideally, a symbolic execution testing system should incorporate a path selection strategy in which the operation of both path selection and symbolic execution is coordinated. Clarke, in the summary of a review paper [Cla85], suggests that

> Symbolic execution is used to guide the selection of paths, which are then symbolically executed. Thus, adaptive systems, where path selection and symbolic execution dynamically interact, should be considered

and

> for the most part, current research is addressing the issues of verification, path selection, test data selection, debugging, optimization and development as independent topics. It is clear, however, that these topics are closely related and eventually should be integrated into a software development environment.

When considering modules the literature over-emphasises the dilemma of choice between macro-expansion and the lemma approach. Macro-expansion increases the size of the program being examined, but provides a more embracing coverage of the software. When maintaining a software system macro-expansion is a particularly useful feature: it allows the impact of a change to be assessed—not just locally, but also throughout the system. When developing a new system the emphasis for symbolic execution may well be on the testing of small well-bounded test units. The choice should be seen as a benefit to be valued rather than as a problem to be overcome.

Arrays are problematic because the static technique of symbolic execution requires information about array subscripts which is often determined dynamically at run-time. Current research sees this as an almost insurmountable difficulty. One solution proposed is to introduce an n-way branch when an ambiguous array reference is encountered, where n is the number of elements in the array. This has the effect of increasing the number of branches significantly and, when branch coverage is being pursued, dramatically increases the number of test cases required such that at least one test case is required for each array element.

Symbolic execution must be capable of determining when constraints on a path are contradictory and hence the path is infeasible. This is usually reported as a problem for symbolic execution, but it may more accurately be regarded as a feature of path selection. Further, it may be argued that symbolic execution is a part of a technique of assessing path feasibility, rather than path infeasibility posing a problem for symbolic execution.

A common approach to assessing path feasibility is to formulate the path condition into an optimization problem. This requires that predicates from the path condition are formulated as constraints suitable for input to optimization software. Predicates of the following forms: $a = b$; $a < b$; $a \leq b$; $a > b$ and $a \geq b$ are all easily formulated into suitable constraints. However, formulation is not straightforward for predicates of the form $a \neq b$. This predicate cannot be passed to an optimizer because of the compound nature of the constraint. Both of the simple constraints $a < b$ and $a > b$ cannot be included in the same system of constraints because they are mutually exclusive and, hence, together they are infeasible.

A second problem facing constraint formulation is the occurrence of strings within predicates: a string cannot be passed to an optimizer because numeric inputs are required.

The occurrence of records in predicates also poses a problem for feasibility checking. Suppose one constraint stipulates equality of two records and a second constraint stipulates the inequality of two variables. When the two variables are fields within the records present in the first constraint, then there is a contradiction between these constraints. Unfortunately, the optimizer will not be able to recognize the contradiction unless the relationship between record and fields is made explicit.

The latter three problems outlined above are not described in the literature and are addressed in more detail in Chapters 6 and 7 in this book.

Weaknesses of specific symbolic execution tools

One of the most glaring weaknesses in the set of existing symbolic execution tools is the absence of a system for commercial data processing languages such as COBOL. Only Howden has referred to the symbolic execution of COBOL programs in his evaluation of several testing techniques [How78b] where, in an experiment, he undertook the symbolic execution of a COBOL program by hand. No researcher has given detailed consideration as to whether this class of software is suitable for symbolic execution or identified particular problems it may possess which would need to be overcome for its successful application. This is surprising, as even in these days of fourth-generation languages COBOL still has a firm place in commercial data processing software development.

As a result of this omission there are several features typical of the software application class which COBOL addresses which are not considered in the literature:

- file handling;
- records in infeasibility checking;
- strings in infeasibility checking;
- high-level string processing constructs.

The literature contains descriptions of thirteen systems that claim to employ symbolic execution. The greatest weakness that these systems exhibit is that six of them do not provide all of the following basic features of a symbolic execution testing system:

- maintaining for each variable an expression in terms of input variables and constants;
- producing a path condition for each path examined;
- determining whether a path condition is feasible.

These three features are fundamental to any tool that is intended to facilitate the application of symbolic execution.

The seven systems that include all three of the basic features have other weaknesses and omissions but there are none common to all seven systems. Three of the six systems, ATTEST, CASEGEN and the FORTRAN testbed, do not deal with assertions.

It may well be coincidence, but all three are systems for analyzing FOR-TRAN programs. EFFIGY, SELECT and IPS process only a small subset of the target language.

Four systems have no path selection strategy. ATTEST requires that paths be input to the system. This is a tedious task. EFFIGY, IPS and SYMBAD cater only for user selection of paths. Both EFFIGY and AT-TEST fail to provide any indication of coverage which is a significant weakness in EFFIGY as the path selection is undertaken interactively.

Ambiguous array references are problematic for two systems. ATTEST simply halts when they are encountered. SELECT generates a branch point with as many exit points as there are elements in the array; thus increasing the number of branches to be covered. SYMBAD maintains a history of the ambiguous array reference. It is not clear how the mechanism handles a branch-point that includes such a reference. CASEGEN maintains the ambiguity until the test data generation, when the causal input variables are given values.

Other weaknesses apply to individual systems. ATTEST detects infeasibility only for systems of linear predicates. Detection of infeasibility in non-linear systems is left to the user. This is surprising for a FORTRAN analyser: one would expect the software to contain non-linear predicates. SELECT is claimed to be an automatic system, yet the user must supply the number of times that loops are to be iterated. CASEGEN does not output the expressions for variables and the path condition. This is unfortunate as they may be useful when debugging.

4.6 The remainder of this book

The primary aim of the work documented in the remainder of this book is to demonstrate that symbolic execution can be usefully applied to commercial data processing software. COBOL is considered representative of this class. The creation of a tool to support the application of a technique is a powerful demonstration that the technique can be applied. The aim was to produce a prototype COBOL symbolic execution testing system as the creation of a full system requires many person-years effort.

For a COBOL program the system should provide the following features:

- maintain for each variable an expression in terms of input variables and constants

- produce a path condition for each path examined;

- determine whether a path condition is feasible;

- incorporate a strategy for automatic path selection;

- allow and facilitate user path selection;

- provide coverage metrics during user path selection;

- cater for ambiguous array references;
- assess path feasibility as each predicate is conjoined to the path condition;
- use the expressions generated by symbolic execution to reduce the selection of infeasible paths;
- verify assertions placed in the source program;
- allow user choice on: macro-expansion versus treating a module call as an input/output boundary.

In the remainder of the book we attempt to:

1. Identify the problems facing the application of symbolic execution to commercial data processing software–in particular to COBOL.

2. Propose a means of overcoming the problems in creating a COBOL symbolic execution testing system.

3. Devise an approach to path selection that selects more useful paths than existing symbolic execution systems and utilises the results of symbolic execution in a bid to reduce the likelihood of selecting infeasible paths.

4. Identify problems facing the use of a linear programming routine to assess the feasibility of paths and to overcome these problems, thus demonstrating the practicality of the technique in a COBOL system.

5. Demonstrate that these proposals are practicable by constructing a prototype symbolic execution testing system for COBOL.

6. Evaluate the symbolic execution testing system that was constructed.

CHAPTER 5

SYM-BOL – a symbolic execution system for COBOL

This chapter provides an overview of the facilities provided by the SYM-BOL system. Chapter 6 describes particular components of the system. Each of these describes the problems presented by COBOL and the means used to overcome them.

5.1 Environment

The SYM-BOL system is written almost exclusively in COBOL 85 and consists of approximately 15 000 lines of source code. Some of the string processing might be more easily implemented in a language such as LISP. However, the bulk of the code in the system is concerned with housekeeping activities for which COBOL is more than adequate. Further, recent additions to COBOL in the 1985 standard, have enhanced its string processing capabilities as well as generally bringing the language more up-to-date.

The system runs on a Microvax 3800 under VMS 5.3. The system is stand-alone, with the exception of testing for path feasibility which uses the NAG-library routine E04MBF. This is a linear optimizer that solves systems of linear constraints provided by the path condition. The feasibility checker is written in FORTRAN. Figure 5.1 shows the system architecture.

5.2 Input

A large subset of standard COBOL can be used. The main restrictions are indexed files, the string manipulation verbs and reference modification.

The primary input to the system is the source program which may contain assertions. Further inputs will be required in response to the results obtained, such as changes to assertions, and the selection of paths to be evaluated.

5.3 Output

- The paths which have been generated;
- Path conditions together with an indication of feasibility including truth of assertions;

- Symbolic expressions for variables;
- Files of test cases ready for execution;
- An indication of branch coverage.

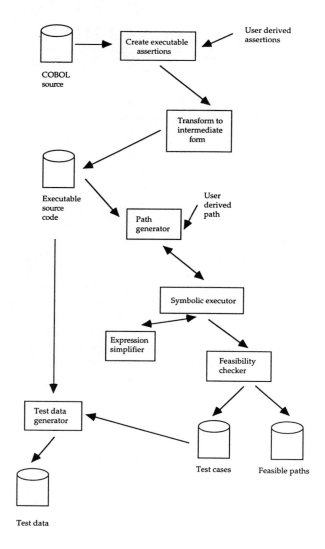

Figure 5.1 *Architecture of the SYM-BOL system.*

5.4 User strategies

It is intended that the SYM-BOL system can be used in a variety of ways. First, it can select a set of paths and generate test cases to cause their execution. Second, it can generate test cases for paths supplied to the system. Third, it can be used as a debugging tool to help locate errors detected by testing. Fourth, it can be used to search out a feasible path for a branch not covered by the testing undertaken so far. Some of these capabilities are not fully implemented; where this is the case it is stated.

5.4.1 Path selection and test data generation

Path selection and test data generation are the main uses of the SYM-BOL system. It can be used to generate paths automatically or, perhaps more usefully, to assist the tester in selecting paths to be tested. Whichever mode of path selection is adopted symbolic execution is undertaken in parallel with the path selection. This allows the results of the symbolic execution to be used to help select the next branch for the path.

In the early versions of SYM-BOL feasibility checking was undertaken only once when the path was complete. This was because the NAG library and associated feasibility checking routines were developed on a Prime 9955, while the rest of the system was developed on a micro-VAX. The feasibility checker has now been transferred on to the micro-VAX and the user may select the frequency of feasibility checking. It may now take place every time a predicate is conjoined to the path condition, or just on completion of the path. There is no practical difficulty in undertaking frequent feasibility checking, as most feasibility assessment appears to be determined after only one or two iterations of the optimizer.

With immediate detection of infeasibility on branch selection the system instantly forces the user or the automatic path selector to make an alternative branch selection. On completion of a feasible path the solution is retained as a test case. The case is stored and may later be transformed into records in the appropriate files ready for test execution of the program.

5.4.2 Test case generation for user supplied paths

Where a particular path has been identified as being of interest, the SYM-BOL system can be used to assess its feasibility and automatically generate test data that causes its execution. For each path the system extracts the path predicates and the assignment statements. The statements on the path are then symbolically executed to produce a path condition and expressions for each of the output variables. The path condition is *not* checked for feasibility as each predicate is added, but is invoked only once when the path condition is complete. This results in faster feasibility checking. When a solution is found the path is feasible and the solution may be used as a test case. The solution is placed as records in the appropriate files making the test execution of the program a simple task. The initial path extraction mechanism, allowing input of source program line numbers, has not yet been implemented and must therefore be undertaken using the 'user path selection' mechanism of the system.

5.4.3 Debugging tool

During testing the user often constructs functional test cases from the knowledge of what the scftware is expected to do. The program is then executed with the test cases using dynamic analysis monitoring facilities. These provide an execution history of the test cases allowing various coverage metrics to be assessed. Additional test cases may then be devised to increase the level of coverage. The program is then executed with the new test cases; the cycle is repeated until the coverage cannot be increased.

When the cause of an error case is easily identified, corrections are made and testing repeated. However, when the cause is not easily pinpointed the SYM-BOL system may be used. The path exercised by the test case which revealed the error is symbolically executed; after the execution of each statement the user is provided with diagnostic output showing the symbolic value of each variable. This information is much more useful than the trace table provided in most COBOL compilation systems because it provides visibility of the expression that yields the erroneous result.

5.4.4 Branch-path location

During the testing process there may be some difficulty in manually deriving test data to execute some branches. Branches which are not covered by previous tests need to be located on a feasible path if they are to be executed. Finding such a feasible path may not always be straightforward, primarily because of the care that needs to be taken in undertaking the search by hand. The system can be used to help in this task by allowing commencement from an existing feasible path.

The strategy employed is to start with the feasible path closest to the branch that is to be executed and then to divert this path to the branch to be included. Automating a repeated search based on existing feasible paths is a relatively difficult process because the number of paths that could be searched is large and there are no obvious search reduction strategies. The first version of the system does not include this feature.

5.4.5 SYM-BOL, 'ideal' and EFFIGY compared

EFFIGY was identified in chapter 4 as a suitable benchmark for assessing future symbolic execution testing systems. The EFFIGY system provides the following features:

- input of source code containing assertions;
- interactive selection of paths;
- output of symbolic values, the truth of assertions together with a statement concerning path feasibility.

SYM-BOL provides all of these features. Additionally, SYM-BOL processes programs written in COBOL, a language more widely used than PL/1, the language processed by EFFIGY. The SYM-BOL system caters for most COBOL features with the exception of indexed files and the string handling verbs. This is in contrast with EFFIGY which processes a comparatively small subset of PL/1.

Two significant factors not listed in Tables 4.1 to 4.4 are the contribution to research and the practicality of the tool. For example, EFFIGY has an advantage over the FORTRAN testbed in terms of contribution to research. EFFIGY includes all the features expected of a symbolic execution testing system, with the exception of test case generation, whereas the FORTRAN testbed does not cater for assertions nor does it incorporate a path selection strategy or provide output of variable expressions and the path condition at each branch point. On the other hand, EFFIGY is not such a generally useful tool as it can be applied only to a limited language subset, whereas the FORTRAN testbed can process the full language specification and it is a commercial product.

SYM-BOL includes all of the features included in EFFIGY. It analyses a language and a class of programs previously ignored by symbolic execution research. However, it is a prototype and in need of much further work before it could become a commercial product.

When SYM-BOL is compared with the seven systems that satisfy the minimum criteria for a symbolic execution system it stands up well. When SYM-BOL is compared with all thirteen of the systems claiming to undertake symbolic execution it appears favourably and is a significant contribution to research in the field. The following brief discussion compares SYM-BOL against only the seven systems that satisfy the minimum criteria and ignores the systems that fail to meet the minimum criteria, except where they contain a useful feature not included in the seven systems.

Path selection in SYM-BOL can be carried out either by user selection or automatically. This is in contrast to ATTEST and the FORTRAN testbed which report no mechanism for path selection other than the input of paths. The remaining systems either provide automatic or user path selection but not both.

When the user is selecting paths SYM-BOL aids the selection by displaying the current expressions for each variable in the branch predicates. This helps the user avoid the selection of obvious infeasible paths; also displayed is a branch coverage measure to help the user select branches not covered by a path. This is not provided by the other systems which allow user selection of paths. IPS and EFFIGY do, however, allow the display of variable expressions at each node.

When the SYM-BOL system is used to automatically generate paths the branch coverage measures and variable expressions are used in an attempt to select feasible paths containing previously uncovered branches. In addition, when faced with otherwise equal choices between branches, the path selection chooses the branch that gives the greatest domain coverage. At present, this domain maximizing selection is rather crude, but it is planned to be developed in a later version. No other symbolic execution testing system incorporates such a strategy. The basis of the approach is that used in SMOTL to determine path feasibility. Minimum and maximum values are maintained for each variable. The branch that provides the greatest distance between the minimum and maximum values is the one selected when, in all other respects, the alternative branches are equally appropriate.

A powerful feature of SYM-BOL's path selection facilities is the interrelationship between the symbolic execution, which creates variable expressions, and the selection of branches for a path. The benefit from this is a reduction in the selection of infeasible paths. Only EFFIGY and IPS provide variable expressions to help the user in making the selection. ATTEST and the FORTRAN testbed have no path selection strategy, specified paths being an input to the system. SELECT and CASEGEN aim for branch coverage, while path selection in EFFIGY, IPS and SYMBAD is solely user driven.

First experiences in using SYM-BOL are that the most useful mode is that involving user selection as this overcomes the branch selection problem of what might be termed 'busy-bottlenecks'. Here, a small number of branches must be executed many times to allow all the branches beyond these points to be executed at least once. Busy-bottlenecks are easily identified and handled by the user, but no method is incorporated within the automatic mode of SYM-BOL – nor any other automatic system – to deal with this problematic, yet common, situation.

When compared to the ideal system described in Chapter 4, SYM-BOL fails to meet the ideal criteria because it can process only COBOL programs and there are some restrictions within the COBOL language. It deals with ambiguous array references by substituting an actual value in place of the input variable index. This is far from satisfactory, but is a practical way of overcoming a difficulty which is caused by the need for a run-time value during a static analysis. SYM-BOL does, however, meet many of the ideal system's requirements. It allows both automatic and interactive use, the source program may contain assertions which can be verified and all of the required outputs with the exception of an idle/active domain report are provided. SYM-BOL also uses the products of symbolic execution to aid path selection in choosing the next branch. This is preferable to making a random branch choice and then testing for feasibility repeatedly until a feasible branch is selected.

5.5 The remainder of this book

This chapter has introduced the SYM-BOL system. The following chapter describes some of its detailed functionality.

- It describes how the system processes assertions placed in the source program. The assertions need not be deleted from the final program. If so desired they may be transparent from the compiler. Alternatively, they can be included in the final executable code.

- describes a series of translations which are made to the COBOL source program. Several stages of translation into simpler standard forms are employed. The final version of the 'source' program is then translated into an intermediate form.

- It explains the approach to path selection and symbolic execution taken. Early systems undertook path selection and symbolic execution in isolation. By synchronizing the two processes the results of symbolic execution are used to help make sensible path selection choices. SYM-BOL uses this co-ordinated approach to path selection in both automatic and user path selection modes.

- It explains why the NAG library linear optimizer E04MBF is suitable for path feasibility checking and how it is used. Two problems, concerning alphanumeric literals (string constants) and implied constraints in record structures are outlined, together with a means of overcoming them.

CHAPTER 6

The main features of SYM-BOL

This chapter examines the main features of the SYM-BOL system with particular emphasis on the handling of assertions, the intermediate form used, path selection and the difficult task of determining path feasibility.

6.1 Assertions

Assertions are used in the axiomatic approach to program proving [Hoa69]. This approach requires that the program validator is able to make statements about the values of variables at various points in the software. Such a statement about what a variable should contain is an assertion.

To prove that the program statements between two points are correct it must be shown that, given the initial assertions are true, the statements up to the end point cause the final assertions to be true. Such a demonstration will have proved partial correctness. Complete correctness requires that it can be shown that the program halts and hence there is no endless loop. To prove a program partially correct requires at least two sets of assertions, one at the beginning and one at the end of a program.

Symbolic execution is able to contribute towards this form of program proving [Han76]. Assertions at any point in a program are conjoined onto the path condition. If the path condition containing the assertions is feasible, then the assertions are upheld. An alternative approach is to negate the assertions before conjoining to the path condition. If the path condition is feasible then the assertions are not upheld. The SYM-BOL system adopts the former approach.

The issue of complete correctness versus partial correctness is not such a major one for symbolic execution because the assessment of correctness is applied to a path. Each path has a terminating point. When an infinite loop exists in the program then the only paths that pass through the loop will be infeasible. Inability to find a feasible path through a loop would suggest that the program is not completely correct.

6.1.1 Specifying assertions in SYM-BOL

Assertions may be included in the source program at any point. The format adopted for their specification is as follows:

```
* assert
*    condition-1


     ⋮
*    condition-n
*end-assert
```

For example in a program processing salaries the initial and final assertions might be as follows:

```
* initial assertions
* assert
* (gross > −1) and
* (gross < 10000) and
* (TaxCode > −1) and
* (TaxCode < 10000)
* end-assert
```

```
* final assertions
* assert
* (state = 'e') or (state = 'n') and
* (tax < gross) or (tax = gross) and
* (ni < gross) or (ni = gross) and
* (tax > 0) or (tax = 0) and
* (ni > 0) or (ni = 0)
* end-assert
```

The assertions are written as comment statements so that normal compilation, linking and execution, are unaffected by their presence. By utilizing the assertion processing option in the SYM-BOL system assertions are transformed into equivalent 'evaluate' statements as follows:

```
* initial assertions
* assert
evaluate true
    when gross > −1 continue
end-evaluate
evaluate true
    when gross < 10000 continue
end-evaluate
evaluate true
    when TaxCode > −1 continue
end-evaluate
evaluate true
    when TaxCode > 1000 continue
```

end-evaluate
* end-assert

* final assertions
* assert
evaluate true
   when $state = \text{‘}e\text{’}$ continue
   when $state = \text{‘}n\text{’}$ continue
end-evaluate
evaluate true
   when $tax < gross$ continue
   when $tax = gross$ continue
end-evaluate
evaluate true
   when $ni < gross$ continue
   when $ni = gross$ continue
end-evaluate
evaluate true
   when $tax > 0$ continue
   when $tax = 0$ continue
end-evaluate
evaluate true
   when $ni > 0$ continue
   when $ni = 0$ continue
end-evaluate
* end-assert

The action of compilation now checks the syntax of both the assertions and the rest of the program. Note that the imperative statement in this form of the assertions is 'continue', no action is taken. When the program contains this version of the assertions the program still executes in the usual way and provides the same results.

Assertions can be used to provide a 'dynamic semantic monitor' by negating the assertions and by changing the resulting 'continue' statements into error messages which report when an assertion violation has occurred.

6.1.2 Assertions and general proofs

When a path containing assertions is found to be feasible the assertions are deemed proven. Unfortunately, the proof is not general because it applies only to the path examined. The same assertions may occur on other paths, yet may not be upheld. To obtain a general proof requires the symbolic execution of all paths between the two points. If these points are the start and end of the program, then this is usually impossible due to the existence of a large, and often infinite, number of paths. This is the perennial path-based testing weakness. To minimize this effect the number of points at which assertions are placed in a program should be increased. The closer the two points between which the proof is attempted the fewer the number of partial-paths that exist between them.

A proof is attempted for all partial-paths between every consecutive pair of sets of assertions. With the exception of the initial and final assertions each set of assertions is used as both initial and final assertions in assessing feasibility of partial-paths.

Consider the program shown below.

Identification Division.
Program-Id. P9a.
Environment Division.
Data Division.
Working-Storage Section.
01 *NiDetails.*
    02 *NiRate*   pic 99v99.
01 *TaxDetails.*
    02 *TaxFree*   pic 9(4)v99.
    02 *TaxRate*   pic 99v9.
    02 *taxable*   pic 9(5)v99.
Linkage section.
01 *InputParameters.*
    02 *gross*   pic 9(5)v99.
    02 *TaxCode*   pic 9(4).
    02 *NiClass*   pic x.
    02 *frequency*   pic x.
        88 *weekly*   value 'w'.
        88 *monthly*   value 'm'.
01 *OutputParameters.*
    02 *state*   picx.
        88 *err*   value 'e'.
        88 *no-error*   value 'n'.
    02 *tax*   pic 9(4)v99.
    02 *ni*   pic 9(3)v99.

Procedure division using
InputParameters OutputParameters.

The-program.
* initial assertions Ai
* assert
* $(gross > -1)$ and

```
*    (gross < 10000) and
*    (TaxCode > −1) and
*    (TaxCode < 10000) and
*    ((NiClass = 'a') or (NiClass = 'b') or (NiClass = 'c')) and
*    ((frequency = 'w') or (frequency = 'm'))
* end-assert

* initialize
      move 'n' to state.

* Set the national insurance rate
evaluate true
      when NiClass = 'a'      move 0.05 to ni − rate
      when NiClass = 'b'      move 0.10 to ni − rate
      when NiClass = 'c'      move 0.15 to ni − rate
      when other              move 0.0 to ni − rate
                              move 'e' to state
                              display 'ni class error'
end-evaluate

* A1
* assert
* ((NiRate > 0) or (NiRate = 0)) and
* (NiRate < 0.2)
* end-assert

* set tax free
if state not = 'e'
then
   if monthly
   then
      compute TaxFree = TaxCode ∗ 10/12 end-compute
   end-if
   if weekly
   then
      compute tax − free = tax − code ∗ 10/52 end-compute
   end-if
   if not monthly and not weekly
   then
      move 0 to TaxFfree
      move 'e' to state
      display 'error in pay period'
   end-if
end-if
```

* A2
* assert
* $((tax - free = 0) \, or \, (tax - free > 0))$ and
* $(tax - free < taxcode)$
* end-assert

* set tax rate
if *state* not= 'e'
then
   compute $taxable = gross - TaxFree$ end-compute
   if $taxable < 10000$
   then
     move 0.3 to *tax-rate*
   else
     if $taxable < 20000$
     then
       move 0.4 to $tax - rate$
     else
       move 0.5 to $tax - rate$
     end-if
   end-if

* A3
* assert
* $(taxable < gross) or (taxable = gross)$ and
* $(tax - rate > 0)$ and
* $(tax - rate < 1)$
* end-assert

* calculate deductions
   compute $ni = NiRate * gross$ end-compute
   compute $tax = TaxRate * taxable$ end-compute
end-if

* final assertions Af
* assert
* $(state = 'e')$ or $(state = 'n')$ and
* $(tax < gross)$ or $(tax = gross)$ and
* $(ni < gross)$ or $(ni = gross)$ and
* $(tax > 0)$ or $(tax = 0)$ and
* $(ni > 0)$ or $(ni = 0)$
* end-assert

Table 6.1 *Reduction of paths.*

Assertion pairs	Number of partial paths
$Ai - A1$	4
$A1 - A2$	9
$A2 - A3$	3
$A2 - Af$	1
$A3 - Af$	1

exit program.
end program *P9a.*

This program has three sets of intermediate assertions as well as initial and final assertions.

Figure 6.1 shows a flowgraph of the program. There are 144 paths through this program. If only initial and final assertions were included all 144 paths would need to be symbolically executed for a proof to have been achieved for the program. The inclusion of intermediate assertions reduces this number significantly as shown in Table 6.1. All intermediate assertions are used as both initial and final assertions thus ensuring connection of all paths from the beginning to the end of the program. All assertion to assertion partial-paths must be symbolically executed, and the final assertions verified correct.

Consider the assertion points $A1$ and $A2$. There are nine partial-paths between these assertion point pairs. All nine partial-paths are symbolically executed and deemed correct. A similar verification is undertaken for assertion point pairs $A2 - A3$, $A2 - Af$ and $Ai - A1$. Because the assertions at $A1$ are used as final assertions in verifying $Ai - A1$, we can be certain that the program is correct at point $A1$. Assertions at $A1$ are also used as initial assertions in verifying $A1 - A2$. This pairing is deemed correct given that $A1$ is correct. We already know that $A1$ is correct from the previous verification stage. This process is repeated for all adjacent assertion point pairs. The result is that all pairs of consecutive assertions are verified and, thus, given that the initial assertions are true, then the program will always satisfy the final assertions.

Looping introduces the problem of termination. Assertions are placed immediately before and immediately after the loop. The difficulty is that there is often a large, even infinite, number of possible iterations. A common approach is to consider a maximum of two iterations together with just one iteration and, in the case of a pre-condition, a zero iteration. On each iteration all possible partial-paths through the loop are verified. For the case containing two iterations this would appear to require the consideration of

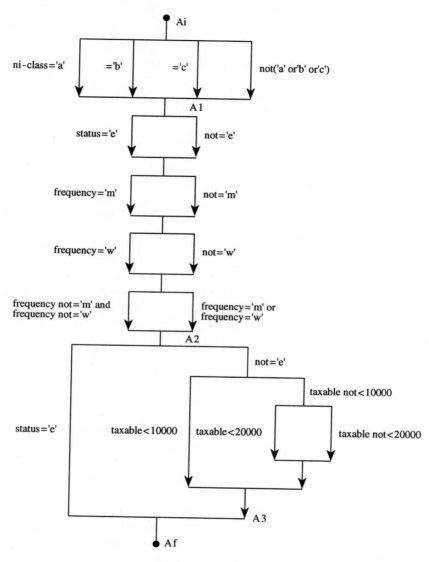

Figure 6.1 *A flowgraph of a program.*

the square of the number of partial paths through the loop. This can be avoided by placing assertions at the beginning of the loop, at the beginning inside the loop and at the end inside the loop. Each iteration of the loop now has a set of initial and final assertions. By making these assertions identical the verification of the final assertions establishes the truth of the initial assertions for the next iteration. In principle two iterations are sufficient to verify the loop.

The key to this approach is that all modified variables on a partial-path must be the subject of strict assertions. An omission will invalidate the verification; so too will weak assertions that are easily satisfied. Provided there are sufficient strict, well placed sets of assertions in a program, symbolic execution is a powerful verification tool.

The SYM-BOL system allows the inclusion of assertions at any point in a program. By selecting the assertion option they are transformed into equivalent COBOL statements. As path selection proceeds, assertions are conjoined to the path condition and, when feasibility checking takes place, are verified. When feasibility checking is requested at every branch it is known immediately which predicate, whether program code or assertion, caused infeasibility. At present the system does not cater for assertion-point to assertion-point verification.

6.1.3 General assertions

The assertions discussed so far are of a simple type such as $a > b$. It is often possible and desirable to express far more wide-ranging assertions than those which just state a relationship between two simple variables. For example the assertion:

$$\forall i : 1 \ldots 100 \bullet a[i] > 0$$

stipulates that all elements of the array 'a' which range from 1 to 100 contain values greater than zero. This can be expressed as a series of simple assertions of the form: $a[1] > 0, a[2] > 0 \ldots$ etc.

It is clearly impractical to expect users of SYM-BOL to write such assertions in such a long form, so a translation from general to specific forms is required as a function in the system.

A similar strategy is adopted for assertions about files. For example:

$$\forall i : 1 \ldots FileSize(file) \bullet file.key[i] < file.key[i + 1]$$

asserts that the file is in ascending order on the field *key*.

Programs containing assertions about many large arrays and files will have a large number of simple assertions, resulting in optimization problems which contain a large number of variables. In comparison with complex optimization problems these are quite straightforward but the concern for a symbolic executor is the response time for feasibility checking. This is not likely to be a problem but further work is required to establish the bounds for acceptable run-time of the system. The current version of SYM-BOL does not cater for general assertions.

6.1.4 Section summary

Three of the seven existing systems, ATTEST, the FORTRAN testbed
and CASEGEN, do not cater for the verification of assertions. Four of
the systems assess path feasibility using optimization techniques; the other
three use theorem provers. Only SELECT uses optimization techniques for
feasibility checking and verifies assertions.

Creation of the SYM-BOL prototype increases to two the number of
systems which use optimization techniques to assess path feasibility and
provide assertion verification, though this is not a particularly significant
combination. Assertions are encoded as comments within the source program. This allows normal compilation and execution to be unaffected by
their presence, yet they are a permanent feature of the program documentation. A simple transformation of the assertions into equivalent COBOL
statements suitable for inclusion on the path condition allows a simple
means of verifying the assertions. Only MALPAS and SYMBAD maintain
assertions as permanent features of the source program.

6.2 Transforming a source program into intermediate form

Symbolic execution is usually achieved by translating a source program into
an intermediate representation which is designed to be more appropriate
than the source program for extracting and symbolically executing a path.

The creation of an intermediate form can be achieved in two ways. First,
it can be created by direct translation from the source program. This requires a complex translator. Second, the source program can undergo several steps of translation into simpler or standard forms in the source language. The final version of the 'source' program is then translated into the
intermediate form by a comparatively simple translator. The SYM-BOL
system uses the second of these two approaches.

This section describes a series of translations which are made to the
COBOL source program. These translations can be grouped into four categories associated with alphanumeric literals, condition names, assignment
constructs and branching constructs. A discussion of alphanumeric literals
is postponed until Section 6.4.1 where it appears as part of the discussion
on formulating path conditions as linear programming problems.

6.2.1 Condition names

A condition name is a high-level means of expressing a conditional expression. Consider the following variable declarations:

```
01   birthday        pic x.
     88   BirthdayPast       value 'p'.
     88   BirthdayToday      value 't'.
```

88   *BirthdayLater*   value '1'.

A conditional statement using a condition name would be of the form:

if *birthday-today*

then

:

This is equivalent to:

if *birthday* = 't'

then

:

Similarly,

set *BirthdayToday* to true

is equivalent to:

move 't' to *birthday.*

To enable conditional statements containing condition names to be treated in the same way as other conditions the simplest approach is to substitute the condition name with the full lower-level condition which it represents, and to transform 'set' statements into equivalent 'move' statements.

6.2.2 Assignment constructs

These can be categorized into: string processing; simple assignments; arithmetic constructs; input statements; and module invocation.

String processing

Simple string manipulation, such as assigning a string to a variable, is carried out using the 'move' construct. COBOL provides the verbs 'inspect', 'string', and 'unstring', together with reference modification, to provide more sophisticated facilities for string manipulation. These more sophisticated facilities are not currently handled by the SYM-BOL system. However, the system does include the use of strings in conditional expressions which are handled in a novel way. This is described later in Section 6.4.1. The system also includes the use of simple string assignments using the 'move' verb. The problems presented by the more sophisticated string manipulation and the means of catering for these in symbolic execution are discussed in Section 6.4.1.

Simple assignments

The COBOL verbs 'move' and 'set' are the facilities provided in COBOL for assigning the contents of one variable to another. 'Move' is adopted as the standard form. The 'set' construct is used for the same purposes as 'move' except that it can be used to act only on index variables and level-88 condition names. Where it is used on index variables the declaration will need to be modified as well as the set statement if it is to be transformed into a move statement. For example consider the following:

```
01   table.
      03   row occurs 100 indexed RowIndex.
            05   field1  pic x.
            05   field2  pic x.
```

set *RowIndex* to 1

To transform the set statement into a move statement also requires the creation of *RowIndex* as an independent data item. The resulting transformation is as follows.

```
01   table.
      03   row occurs 100.
            05   field1 pic x.
            05   field2 pic x.
01   RowIndex pic 999.
```

move 1 to *RowIndex*

Arithmetic constructs

The COBOL verbs 'add', 'subtract', 'multiply', 'divide', 'compute', 'set', and, arguably, 'perform varying' are provided in COBOL for evaluating arithmetic expressions and assigning the result to a variable. All of these can be expressed using 'compute'. For example consider:

```
perform varying a from 1 by 1 until a = 10
   code
end-perform
```

is transformed to:

```
move 1 to a
perform until a = 10
   code
   compute a = a + 1
end-perform
```

Input statements

'Accept' and 'read' are the facilities provided in COBOL for the input of data into variables. 'Accept' is used to set input variables interactively and 'read' is used to extract data from files. No standard form is adopted for this group. During symbolic execution both 'read' and 'accept' cause the assignment of a new symbolic value.

Module invocation

The COBOL verb 'call' is the means of invoking a sub-program. The verb 'sort' could also be included in this class. Although it is a COBOL provided facility, 'sort' behaves in much the same way as 'call'. Invoking 'sort' requires the passing of a file and the return of a new file.

When treating a module call as an output-input statement the returned results are given new symbolic values. 'Call' can be treated as an output-input statement or as a 'perform' which causes symbolic execution to continue into the called routine. 'Sort' is always treated as an output-input statement.

6.2.3 Branching constructs

The transformations made to branching constructs are necessary to facilitate the creation of a path condition and its subsequent feasibility checking. Path conditions are made up of a set of conjoined predicates which are taken from the conditions at each branch point on a path. When the condition is a simple two-way selection, either the predicate expressed in the condition (the true branch) or the negation of the predicate expressed in the condition (the false branch) is conjoined to the path condition. The predicates that make up the path condition are used to form a set of constraints in a linear programming problem which is submitted to an optimizer.

Simple conditions

It is a simple matter to formulate simple equalities into a constraint appropriate for submission to an optimizer. However, it is a little more difficult to formulate the negated condition into suitable constraints.

For example, consider the condition if $a = b$. The predicate for the true branch is $a = b$, while the predicate for the false branch is: $a \neq b$.

The predicate for the true branch can be passed to an optimizer, but the predicate for the false branch cannot. The only way of passing a negated condition to the optimizer is to express it as an alternative compound condition $a < b \lor a > b$. However, if both of these constraints are passed to the optimizer, then the problem will not be solvable due to a contradiction in the constraints. Each of the predicate components are implicitly separate branches.

One way of overcoming this difficulty is to transform all apparently two-way selections into three-way selections, each branch representing one of the three possible predicates that can be passed as a constraint to the optimizer. For example:

if $a = b$		evaluate true
then		when $a < b$ s2
$\quad$ s1	can be expressed as:	when $a = b$ s1

else   when $a > b$ s2
   s2   end-evaluate
end-if

Each of the three constraints $a < b, a = b$ and $a > b$ can be successfully passed to an optimizer as a constraint on a path condition.

Compound conditions

Where the predicates contain Boolean operators forming compound conditions a similar problem arises to the problem of false branches in a simple condition. There is no difficulty when a branch predicate contains only the Boolean operator.

Here, the component conditions of the compound condition are treated as individual predicates and constitute two or more constraints. However, the negation of this compound condition cannot be passed as a constraint. Consider the conditional statement:

if $a = b$ and $c = d$
then
   s1
else
   s2
end-if

The true branch predicate: $a = b \land c = d$ can be conjoined to the path condition and passed to the optimizer as constraints $a = b$ and $c = d$. The false branch predicate $\neg(a = b \land c = d)$ which can be expressed alternatively as $a \neq b \lor c \neq d$ cannot be passed as a constraint. One approach is to decompose the compound condition to produce nested if statements which in turn can be transformed into **evaluate** statements containing appropriate constraints. For example:

if $a = b$
then
   if $c = d$
   then
      s1
   else
      s2
   end-if
else
   s2
end-if

can be transformed to:

evaluate true
   when $a = b$

```
evaluate true
    when c > d    s2
    when c < d    s2
    when c = d    s1
end-evaluate
when a > b s2
when a < b s2
end-evaluate
```

An alternative approach is to use a single evaluate statement which is, essentially, a form of truth table:

```
evaluate true also true
    when a < b also c < d       s2
    when a = b also c < d       s2
    when a > b also c < d       s2
    when a < b also c = d       s2
    when a = b also c = d       s1
    when a > b also c = d       s2
    when a < b also c > d       s2
    when a = b also c > d       s2
    when a > b also c > d       s2
end-evaluate
```

Each of the when clauses forms part of a path condition which can be passed to an optimizer as a system of constraints. There is no need for further negation of conditions to take place: all possible conditions are explicitly specified in the newly constructed evaluate statements.

An alternative to transformation into nested simple conditions and truth tables requires the maintenance of several path conditions for each path. The precise number of path conditions varies with the number of *or* operators. At the point on the path where a compound condition containing *or* is encountered the maintenance of two or more path conditions is commenced. The first path condition contains the simple condition before the *or* operator, the second path condition contains the simple condition after the *or* operator. This approach has the benefit that it maintains the structure of the program that was created by the programmer.

Having multiple path conditions for each path increases the number that are to be checked for feasibility. This is no worse than creating additional paths by expanding the compound conditions. However, there is an overhead in applying this technique. The symbolic execution component of the testing system must maintain the connections between the multiple path conditions and their paths, whereas the use of compound condition expansion needs no such mechanism and a dynamic analysis coverage monitor can be used to assess the impact of the testing.

The SYM-BOL system is designed to use compound condition expansion to deal with conditions containing the 'or' logical operator.

when other *exit from multi-branch conditionals*

Consider the following program fragment:

```
evaluate true
   when x = a    s1
   when x = b    s2
   when other    s3
end-evaluate
```

The predicates for the first two cases are straightforward, they are $x = a$ and $x = b$. The third case is more complex being $x \neq a$ and $x \neq b$. This compound condition is transformed in a manner similar to that described above for compound conditions. The following shows an appropriate transformation:

```
evaluate true
   when x = a   s1
   when x = b   s2
   when x < a
   evaluate true
      when x < b      s3
      when x > b      s3
   end-evaluate
   when x > a
   evaluate true
      when x < b      s3
      when x > b      s3
   end-evaluate
end-evaluate
```

When the conditions in the multi-branch construct contain constants the transformation can be to a simpler form. Consider the following program fragment:

```
evaluate true
   when x = 'a'     s1
   when x = 'c'     s2
   when other       s3
end-evaluate
```

The following shows its simpler transformation:

```
evaluate true
```

```
    when x = 'a'              s1
    when x = 'c'              s2
    when x < 'a'              s3
    when x > 'a' and x <'c'   s3
    when x > 'c'              s3
end-evaluate
```

This transformation requires all missing domains to be included in the list of alternatives. This is easily achieved by arranging the constants in a sort sequence allowing easy specification of the domain constraints. It may be that some of the derived domains are empty. Consider the declaration 01 x pic x. Now consider the domain defined as: when $x > $ 'a' and $x < $ 'b'. This is empty and can be deleted.

Iterations

Iterations of the form:

```
perform test before until a = b
   s1
end-perform
```

give rise to conditions which provide constraints for inclusion on the path condition. This may be achieved by transforming into the following form.

```
iter1.
evaluate true
   when a < b continue
   when a = b go end-iter1
   when a > b continue
end-evaluate
s1
go iter1.
end-iter1.
```

Should the loop be of the form: perform test after until $a = b$, the statements at line 8 are moved to line 2. Where the condition is a compound condition the transformation is of the same form, but in this case has two evaluate statements.

Compute–on size error–not on size error

Many statements contain branches which can be converted to the evaluate standard form. For example, in the following program fragment, by using the picture declaration of variable a to provide the maximum value allowed for a the 'size error' clauses in

```
a        pic 99.
b        pic 99.
c        pic 99.
compute a = b + c
   size error        s1
   not size error   s2
end-compute
```

to be transformed to:

```
a        pic 99.
b        pic 99.
c        pic 99.
compute a = b + c
evaluate true
   when b + c < 99      s2
   when b + c = 99      s2
   when b + c > 99      s1
end-evaluate
```

Read—at end—not at end

Input and output statements also contain branching. Consider the following program fragment:

```
data division.
file section.
fd Fain record varying depending wa-length.
01   Farec        pic x(50).
working-storage section.
01   Walength     pic 9(5) comp.
01   Wain         pic x(50).
procedure division.
The-program.
read Fain into Wain
   end        s1
   not end    s2
end-read
s3
```

To transform this into the evaluate standard form requires the use of declarative sections to remove the 'end' and 'not end' clauses. Statements in the declarative sections are not conjoined onto the path condition. The transformed program fragment is then:

```
data division.
file section.
fd Fain record varying depending WaLength.
```

```
01   FaRec         pic x(50).
working-storage section.
01   WaLength      pic 9(5) comp.
01   Wain          pic x(50).
01   EndOfFile     pic s9(9) comp value external rmseof.
procedure division.
declaratives.
Dvfain section.
  use after standard exception procedure on FaIn.
end declaratives.
Theprogram.
read FaIn into WaIn
evaluate true
    when rmssts of FaIn = EndOfFile      s1
    when rmssts of FaIn< EndOfFile       s2
    when rmssts of FaIn> EndOfFile       s2
end-evaluate
s3
```

Test data generation

The solution to a path condition provides a test case that will cause execution of the path. The test case can be in one of three forms: file only input, interactive only input or both file and interactive input.

For test cases that are wholly read from files the system generates the necessary files containing the data values produced during feasibility checking: the program is simply executed and no further user intervention is required.

When the test case is wholly input interactively by the user the test cases are placed in a file in000.dat. The file contains, in the order of input, the variable name and its data value. At present this file is listed and used as a note pad when executing the program.

For hybrid file and interactive input test cases both the necessary files and in000.dat are created. During execution the user inputs the interactive inputs and the rest of the data is read from the files as usual.

Intermediate form

The developer of the software under test is not required to examine the transformed source program. It is an intermediate representation used during path selection and symbolic execution. However, both forms can be compiled and executed and will produce equivalent results.

This approach has the advantage of allowing the creation of a comparatively simple translator from source program to intermediate form which is useful for a prototype development, allowing easy incremental inclusion of language constructs.

6.2.4 Section summary

The creation of an intermediate form can be achieved either by direct translation from the source program or by several steps of translation from the source into simpler or standard forms in the source language. The final version of the 'source' program is then translated into the intermediate form. The SYM-BOL system uses the second of these two approaches. COBOL has a wide variety of both assignment and branching statements. The core of the translation strategy is the use of three standard forms, one each for arithmetic, input and branching statements.

The first-stage intermediate form is a COBOL program with dramatically reduced statement variety. This form can be compiled and run giving identical results to the original program. This is then translated into the final stage intermediate form similar to that found in other systems. This two stage approach has the benefit for a prototype system of allowing the development of a stable COBOL-to-intermediate-form translator, while allowing easy inclusion of an additional COBOL feature by the introduction of a new routine in the first-stage translator which just translates the new COBOL feature into the standard form.

Most of the earlier systems do not undertake the translation into intermediate form in the two stage manner employed by SYM-BOL. Introducing additional language features is thus likely to be a little more difficult in these systems though not a significant problem. The SPADE system is an exception, translating the source program into an intermediate form that could be described as a specification language. This form must be further translated into a form suitable for path extraction and symbolic execution. It has the advantage of providing a common intermediate form for many program languages; thus development of a tool for another language is eased at the expense of some additional translation for each language. The approach used in SPADE has the further disadvantage of providing output that refers to the specification language, which is further from the source program than is the COBOL standard form from its source program.

6.3 Path selection and symbolic execution

The problem of determining what input data is required to execute a path is in some ways more difficult for COBOL-based systems intended for commercial file processing than for systems based on other languages such as FORTRAN which are intended for numerical algorithms. The reason for this is that when a symbolic executor is used in a commercial data processing environment a path requires the reading of records from files. This means that a test case becomes a set of files of records, rather than just several numerical values. On the other hand, the path conditions may be simpler than for numerical algorithms which can contain complex predicates.

In a commercial file processing program a single path can give almost complete branch coverage and, furthermore, will cause the processing of many records from several files. There will be many symbolic values generated during symbolic execution of such a path and the ordering of these values is critical to the execution of the path.

6.3.1 Path selection

The term 'path selection' is adopted in favour of the more common 'path generation'. 'Selection' implies a degree of care not suggested by 'generation' which implies an almost random choice.

Path selection version 1

In the early stage of development the only method of path selection in the SYM-BOL system was a simple user selection at each branch point. The user is presented with the alternative branch predicates and makes a selection. The appropriate predicate is placed on the straight-line form of the path followed by the statements on the branch. This is repeated for each branch in turn until an exit is reached.

The straight-line form of the path is then symbolically executed using forward expansion to produce variable expressions and the path condition. The completed path condition is checked for feasibility. While this method works, it became clear that many of the causes of infeasible paths could be avoided if the user had visibility of the expressions for the variables in the predicates being considered. To achieve this visibility symbolic execution must be performed in step with path selection rather than at the culmination of path selection.

Path selection version 2

At each branch point the predicates for each branch are displayed together with the current expression for each variable in the predicates. The user can now see that some of the predicates are clearly infeasible. For example:

Node 006 on Path 002

1   002 $J = I$
2   000 $J > I$
3   001 $J < I$

Current expression for J
$A@01 + 5$

Current expression for I
$A@01$

In this case it is clear that branches 1 and 3 are infeasible and branch 2 is feasible. An additional aid is the provision of the branch coverage count, 002, 000, 001 in the example. If all the branches were feasible the user may choose to select branch 2 as it has not yet been covered.

Where the expressions are too complicated for the user to make a quick judgement on the feasibility by inspection, a branch may be chosen based on the branch coverage, or even at random. The system then assesses its feasibility. When an infeasible choice is made the expressions are redisplayed and an alternative branch is chosen. This is repeated until a feasible branch is identified.

In some cases the expressions are constants. For example:

Node 007 on Path 002

1   002 $X = Z$
2   000 $X > Z$
3   001 $X < Z$

Current expression for X
5

Current expression for Z
5

Here the only feasible branch is branch 1. The system now makes this choice without presenting it to the user. The predicate is not conjoined to the path condition as it is true and therefore redundant.

6.3.2 Automatic path selection

By utilizing the current expressions for the variables and the branch coverage data an automatic path selector has been created. First, predicates which are obviously infeasible are removed from consideration. Second, the branch coverage value is used to select the least covered of the remaining branches. However, this strategy is flawed. Many of the uncovered parts of a program may require passage through a well exercised branch before they can be reached.

For this form of automatic path selection to be successful, the forward expansion approach must be partly abandoned and replaced by a strategy that commences at an uncovered branch. Path selection now works forward from this point in the usual way and backward to the beginning of the program. This 'uncovered-branch-out' approach has not been implemented in the SYM-BOL system, partly because it requires the addition of a backward substitution symbolic executor and partly because there is another promising alternative for automatic path selection based on domains. This is described in this section.

Over the past few years, researchers have been considering the problem of what constitutes a good test. This work has resulted in the use of domains as a means of creating test cases [Whi80]. Where a test case can be considered to represent a large set of possible test cases, then it can be seen as a better test case than one which is representative of only a small number of possible cases.

The SYM-BOL system is designed to incorporate a path selection strategy in which the expressions produced by the symbolic execution are utilised in an attempt to identify 'interesting' paths. For example, a path which constrains variables less than another path is potentially more important to the tester because a larger domain has been examined. The basis of the strategy is to maximize the coverage of each variable's domain.

Active and idle domains

Consider the COBOL variable declared as follows:

01 a pic S999.

This declaration specifies the domain of the variable. It may take on values from: -999 to 999. Its domain may be expressed as:$-1000 < a < 1000$. For a particular path the path condition may be:$-10 < a < 25$ It is clear that the domain of the variable A on the path is constrained to a small subset of the domain of the variable. This may be termed the **active domain** of variable a. The non-covered parts of the domain, which may be termed the **idle domain** is: $-1000 < a < -9 \land 24 < a < 1000$. If further paths exist which would transfer all or part of an idle variable domain to an active variable domain, then they should be included in the test set. There is a risk that this strategy will produce a large number of paths. Thus, the strategy of the path selector will need to incorporate a means of choosing branches that minimize the size of idle variable domains.

A path that minimizes the idle domain for one variable is unlikely to have the same effect on all other input variables on the same path. A compromise here may be to determine both the sum of the minimum values of the input variables and the sum of the maximum values of the input variables covered so far at each conditional statement. The branch that provides the greatest range between minimum and maximum sums of input variables is the branch selected for inclusion on the path being generated.

Once complete branch coverage has been achieved, the variable ranges would then be examined for idleness. Further paths may be selected to reduce the size of idle domains. A final refinement requires that the set of paths is now reduced, where possible, to decrease the number of paths without decreasing coverage or increasing idleness. The first version of the SYM-BOL system uses only a simple domain coverage strategy when selecting paths and does not attempt to minimise the idle domain sizes once the paths have been created.

User-based path selection vs automatic path selection

Indications so far suggest that the goal of automatic path selection is difficult to achieve if good selection decisions are to be made. A skilled (and even a not so skilled) software tester will devise better tests than the automatic selection approaches described here and elsewhere. The difficulty facing the tester when selecting paths and creating test cases is an administrative one. For example, it is difficult to: keep track of expressions for variables and path conditions; determine path feasibility; generate test cases to satisfy the path condition; create the files of test cases and execute interactive programs with the intended inputs.

The most useful software testing tools will be those that give the greatest support to the tester rather than those that are intended to replace the tester. The SYM-BOL system can be used in either capacity but the supporting role looks the more promising.

6.3.3 Section summary

In some of the earlier systems (ATTEST, CASEGEN, FORTRAN testbed) path selection and symbolic execution are undertaken in isolation. First, a path or set of paths is identified. Second, the paths are symbolically executed to produce a path condition. As each branch predicate is conjoined to the path condition the new partial path condition is passed to either a theorem prover or an optimizer to assess whether the path is feasible. This approach is useful as it identifies the point at which the path becomes infeasible and allows the selection of an alternative branch without the need for recommencing the path selection from the entry point. However, what the approach lacks is the ability to avoid selecting the branch that causes infeasibility in the first place. A simple inspection is often sufficient to show that a branch predicate would cause infeasibility.

The SYM-BOL system integrates path selection and symbolic execution allowing the current variable expressions and the branch coverage measures to be used in path selection. This helps achieve branch coverage and also reduces the selection of infeasible paths. Both EFFIGY and IPS also provide output of the path condition and variable expressions allowing the user to avoid selection of obviously infeasible paths.

SYM-BOL provides both user and automatic path selection modes, the integrated path selection and symbolic execution being used in both modes of operation. First indications are that the most useful mode is user selection as this overcomes the branch selection problem of what may be called 'busy bottlenecks', where a small number of branches must be executed many times to allow all the branches beyond these points to be executed at least once. Busy bottlenecks are easily identified and handled by the user, but no method is incorporated within the automatic mode of SYM-BOL, or any other automatic system, to deal with this situation. Interestingly, neither EFFIGY nor IPS provide automatic path selection.

6.4 Determining path feasibility and test generation

The identification of feasible and infeasible paths is central to the path-based approach to testing. There are two approaches to determining infeasibility: axiomatic and algebraic [Cla81].

The axiomatic technique makes use of a theorem proving system which determines whether the constraints are contradictory [Man73]. The algebraic technique uses the simple conditions within the path condition as a set of constraints which the system attempts to solve. SYM-BOL uses the algebraic technique.

When using the algebraic approach an artificial objective function is created, for example, the sum of the variables present in the predicates. An optimizer is then used in an attempt to minimise the objective function subject to the constraints. The objective function selected does not appear to affect whether a solution can be found, only the nature of the solution. Non-linear sets of constraints for a path are problematic as there is no assurance that a solution can be found even though the constraints are not in conflict. Linear systems of constraints do not pose this problem and output from a linear optimizer will be in one of two forms. The first is a solution, in which case the path is feasible. The solution may be used as a test case to execute the path. The second is a message indicating that the constraints are contradictory; hence, the path is infeasible.

White and Cohen [Whi80] have identified commercial data processing software as a class of software for which non-linear constraints are unlikely to pose a problem. They report that in a study of 50 COBOL programs from data processing applications the most important result was that only one predicate out of the 1225 tabulated was non-linear. They conclude: 'we believe the sample is large enough to indicate that non-linear predicate interpretations are rarely encountered in data processing applications.' This may be because commercial data processing rarely requires squaring, cubing and higher order functions.

In an analysis of COBOL programs [Alj79] the ADD verb accounted for 73.5% of all arithmetic statements. The verb that facilitates squaring and cubing is COMPUTE. In the study COMPUTE accounted for only 3.2% of all arithmetic statements. Unfortunately, no analysis of the use of the COMPUTE verb was given but it seems reasonable to assume that only a small proportion of the arithmetic statements contained squaring, cubing or higher order functions. If this is general, then the occurrence of non-linear predicates is likely to be negligible.

White and Cohen concluded: 'It is clear that any testing strategy restricted to linear predicates is still viable in many areas of programming practice'. Systems, such as symbolic executors, which can determine infeasibility by using linear optimizers will be useful for a large number of programs and, in particular, for commercial data processing applications.

6.4.1 The problem of the alphanumeric literal and the linear optimizer

Formulating the path predicates into a problem suitable for a linear optimizer is a relatively straightforward matter for numerical programs, where predicates tend to consist only of operators, numeric variables and numeric constants. Commercial data processing software, on the other hand, contains an additional class of predicate component – the alphanumeric. Constraints that contain only numeric variables, numeric constants and alphanumeric variables, but not alphanumeric literals can be processed by a numerical optimizer treating all variables as numeric. The solution will not necessarily be a natural test case but its feasibility will have been assessed. The problematic path condition is the one that contains alphanumeric literals which cannot sensibly be passed to an optimizer which requires numeric data.

There are two alternative approaches to overcoming this problem. The first is for each alphanumeric literal in a predicate to create a numeric token. This is then passed, along with the variables and constants, to the optimizer. The second solution is to separate the predicates of the path condition into two categories: those containing alphanumeric literals and variables and those not containing alphanumerics. Then, formulate the numeric predicates into an optimization problem and pass to an optimizer. The alphanumeric predicates are now evaluated by a specially written routine.

Both of these approaches rely on the fact that predicates containing alphanumeric variables are independent of the predicates containing numeric variables. This is clearly true, as it is meaningless to compare an alphanumeric variable with a numeric variable. Of course, the value of an alphanumeric variable may, at some stage, determine the value of a numeric variable such as a condition based on an alphanumeric variable where one branch modifies a numeric variable, but this is taken in to account by the symbolic execution of the path.

Consider the following fragment of code:

```
1    begin-example.
2      accept ST1
3      accept ST2
4      accept A
5      if A > 15
6      then
7         compute C = C + 1
8      else
9         if ST1 = 'X'
10        then
11           compute B = B + 2
12        else
13           compute B = B + 1
14        end-if
15     end-if
16     if A < 10
17     then
18        compute D = D + 1
19     end-if
20     if ST2 = 'Y'
21     then
22        compute C = C + 2
23     end-if
24     if ST1 = ST2
25     then
26        compute D = B + C
27     end-if
28     stop run.
29     end program example.
```

There are many paths through this program fragment. Consider the following path: 1, 2, 3, 4, 5, 8, 9, 10, 11, 14, 15, 16, 19, 20, 21, 22, 23, 24, 25, 26, 27, 28. The statements on this path, and the evolving path condition as it is symbolically executed by forward expansion, are

Statement	Path Condition
2 accept $ST1$	
3 accept $ST2$	
4 accept A	
5 [not $A > 15$]	$\neg A > 15$
9 [$ST1 = $ 'X']	$\neg A > 15 \wedge ST1 = $ 'X'

11 compute $B = B + 2$

16 [not $A < 10$] $\neg A > 15 \land ST1 = $ 'X' $\land \neg A < 10$

20 [$ST2 = $'Y'] $\neg a > 15 \land ST1 = $ 'X' $\land \neg A < 10 \land ST2 = $'Y'

22 compute $C = C + 2$

24 [ST1 = ST2] $\neg A > 15 \land ST1 = $ 'X' $\land \neg A < 10 \land ST2 = $'Y',
$ST1 = ST2$

26 compute $D = B + C$

Alternative 1–The numeric token approach

Substitute 'X' by 1 and 'Y' by 2 giving the new set of constraints:

$\neg A > 15 \land ST1 = 1 \land \neg A < 10 \land ST2 = 2 \land ST1 = ST2$

All the path constraints are now submitted to the numerical optimizer where the problem cannot be solved, hence the path is infeasible.

Suppose now that the condition on line 24 had read: if $ST1 > ST2$. The constraints would now be:

$\neg A > 15 \land ST1 = $'X'$\land \neg A < 10 \land ST2 = $ 'Y' $\land ST1 > ST2$

Substitute 'X' by 5 and 'Y' by 2 giving the new set of constraints:

$\neg A > 15 \land ST1 = 5 \land \neg A < 10 \land ST2 = 2 \land ST1 > ST2$

This is solvable yet the path is infeasible. The introduction of a simple rule overcomes the difficulty: numerical tokens must give the same sort sequence as the literals they represent. Applying this rule would mean that tokens to represent 'X' and 'Y' must reflect the relationship 'X' < 'Y', the tokens 5 and 2 violate this principle. Changing the values to say, 4 and 6 respectively, overcomes the problem giving constraints of:

$\neg A > 15 \land ST1 = 4 \land \neg A < 10 \land ST2 = 6 \land ST1 > ST2$

which is infeasible.

Alternative–2 The alphanumeric constraint solver

Here we separate the path constraints into two classes.

numeric   **alphanumeric**

N1 $\neg A > 15$ A1 $ST1 = $ 'X'

N2 $\neg A < 10$ A2 $ST2 = $ 'Y'

                          A3 $ST1 = ST2$

The numeric constraints are input to a numerical optimizer and yield a solution. The right hand sides of A1 and A2 are substituted into A3 giving A4 'X' = 'Y' Clearly this expression is contradictory. The path is thus infeasible.

The case above is trivial. The approach is useful only if it is practical for larger sets of constraints. Consider the following set of constraints:

1. $AN1 > \text{`X'}$
2. $AN2 < \text{`Y'}$
3. $AN3 = \text{`Z'}$
4. $AN1 > AN2$
5. $AN3 = AN4$
6. $AN4 = AN2$

For each equality containing a variable on one side of the equality substitute the expression on the other side into all other constraints containing the variable. Duplicate constraints should not be introduced. Several passes through the constraints should be made until no new constraints can be created. The substitution should terminate as soon as a contradictory constraint is produced. This is shown below

3. in 5. gives	7.	$\text{`Z'} = AN4$
5. in 6. gives	8.	$AN3 = AN2$
6. in 2. gives	9.	$AN4 < \text{`Y'}$
6. in 4. gives	10.	$AN1 > AN4$
3. in 8. gives	11.	$\text{`Z'} = AN2$
5. in 9. gives	12.	$AN3 < \text{`Y'}$
5. in 10. gives	13.	$AN1 > AN3$
7. in 9. gives	14.	`Z'} < \text{`Y'

Constraint 14 is contradictory so the path is infeasible. On completion of repeated substitution from equalities contradictions may not have been detected although they are present. Substitution from inequalities must then be undertaken e.g.

1. $AN1 > \text{`X'}$
2. $AN2 < \text{`X'}$
3. $AN1 < AN2$

1. in 2. gives 4. $AN2 < AN1$
3. in 4. gives 5. $AN2 < AN2$

Constraint 5 is contradictory, hence the path is infeasible.

Many substitutions may be necessary before feasibility is assured. An assessment of the maximum number of substitutions possible shows the potential size of the problem.

The number of variables and literals (operands) determines the maximum number of constraints. For two operands there are four possible constraints: $<, >, =$ and $\leq$. Where constraints consist solely of two operands then the maximum number of constraints possible $MCon$ is given by:

$$MCon = (n(n-1)/2) * 4 = 2n(n-1)$$

where n is the number of operands. The maximum number of substitutions is given by:

$$MSub = m(m-1)/2$$

where m is the number of constraints.

By substituting *Max Con* the maximum number of substitutions is:

$$MaxSub = 2n(n-1)(2n(n-1)-1)/2 = n(n-1)(2n(n-1)-1)$$

which is

$$= 2n^4 - 4n^3 + n^2 + n$$

where n is the number of operands. Experience suggests that most condition statements containing alphanumeric literals contain the operators $=$ and $\leq$, but rarely, $<$ and $>$. This reduces the number of substitutions but does not affect the rate of increase.

Where either side of an inequality may contain expressions of more than one operand the maximum number of substitutions rises even faster.

The creation of a strategy to solve this problem faces the same difficulties as the solution of linear programming problems, with the additional difficulty of not being able to manipulate the constraints in a straightforward fashion.

The construction of a special routine to deal with alphanumeric literals appears to be impractical. Further research into the nature of path constraints would be needed to establish that the number of operands present in the conditions of most paths is small and that the substitutions required are small in comparison with the potential number.

Alternative 1 using numeric tokens is the approach implemented in the SYM-BOL system and it appears to work in practice.

6.4.2 Record and group items

A further requirement that must be satisfied to enable the use of linear optimizers for assessing path feasibility concerns the comparison of records with different component structures. Consider the following record declarations.

```
01   A.
     02  B        pic XXX.
     02  C        pic XX.


01   D.
     02  E        pic X.
     02  F        pic XX.
     02  G        pic XX.
```

Suppose a path has constraints:

$$A = D \wedge C \neq G.$$

When attempting to solve these constraints the solver must be supplied with the relationship between A and C and between D and G. This can be achieved by submitting only elementary items to the solver. In this case the constraints would be:

$$B + C = E + F + G \wedge C \neq G.$$

This is still inadequate. Components that are individually compared need to be isolated giving constraints of:

$$B = E + F \wedge C = G \wedge C \neq G.$$

This is adequate to identify the contradiction.

6.4.3 Formulating LP constraints

Each of the when clauses in the evaluate statement consists of a simple condition. Each simple condition is of one of the forms $A = B \wedge A < B \wedge A > B$. In optimization problems it is usual to reformat constraints such as $A = B$ into a zero term form, for example, $A - B = 0$.

The optimizer used by the authors for development work requires constraints to be expressed with both lower and upper bounds. Thus $A = B$ would be expressed a $0 \leq A - B \leq 0$

Inequalities are expressed in a similar manner. To express the simple condition $X < 0$ as $X \leq?$ a negative number close to zero is used: -1.0E-21. To express $X > 0$ as $X \geq?$ a positive number close to zero is used: +1.0E- 21. Where there is no lower or upper bound, extremely small or extremely large values are used. These are -1.0E+21 and +1.0E+21. The inequalities would be reformatted as follows: $A < B$ would be reformatted as $-1.0E + 21 \leq A - B \leq -1.0E - 21$, $A > B$ would be reformatted as $+1.0E - 21 \leq A - B \leq +1.0E + 21$ or alternatively as $-1.0E + 21 <= B - A <= -1.0E - 21$.

Variable declarations provide implicit constraints. So for example if A is declared as A pic 9, this would be formulated as a general constraint $0 \leq A \leq 9$

The optimizer used for development work does not make the input of an objective function mandatory. Where it is omitted the first feasible solution is returned that is ideal for the purpose of feasibility checking. For a routine that requires an objective function, any expression involving all the variables on the path condition will suffice, for example, the sum of these variables.

6.4.4 An example

Consider the program below. Applying the transformations described above to this program yields the program that follows it.

Identification Division.

Program-id. triangle.
Environment Division.
Input-Output Section.
File-Control.
select $FaIn$ assign to 'tri.dat'.
Data Division.
File Section.
fd $FaIn$ record varying depending $WaLength$.
01   FaInput   pic x(3).
Working-Storage Section.
01    $WaIn$.
    03 I pic 9.
    03 J pic 9.
    03 K pic 9.
01    $WaLength$ pic 9 comp value 3.
01    $WaEof$ pic x.
01    $TriMatch$ pic 9.
Procedure Division.
begin-triangle.
open input $FaIn$
read $FaIn$ into $WaIn$
  end
    move 'y' to $WaEof$
  not end
    move 'n' to $WaEof$
  end-read
perform test before until $WaEof$ = 'y'
  if $I + J > K$ and $J + K > I$ and $K + I > J$
  then
    move 0 to $TriMatch$
    if $I = J$
    then
      compute $TriMatch = TriMatch + 1$
    end-if
    if $J = K$
    then
      compute $TriMatch = TriMatch + 1$
    end-if
    if$K = I$
    then
      compute $TriMatch = TriMatch + 1$
    end-if
    evaluate true
      when $TriMatch = 0$ display 'Scalene'

```
            when TriMatch = 1 display 'Isosceles'
            when TriMatch = 3 display 'Equilateral'
            when other display 'Error'
          end-evaluate
        else
          display 'Not a Triangle'
        end-if
        read FaIn into WaIn
        end
            move 'y' to WaEof
        end-read
    end-perform
    close FaIn
    stop run.
    end program triangle.
```

The transformed program is:

```
Identification Division.
Program-id. triangle.
Environment Division.
Input-Output Section.
File-Control.
        select FaIn assign to 'tri.dat'.
Data Division.
File Section.
fd FaIn record varying depending WaLength.
01   fa − input          pic x(3).
Working-Storage Section.
01   WaIn.
        03   I           pic 9.
        03   J           pic 9.
        03   K           pic 9.
01   WaLength            pic 9 comp value 3.
01   WaEof               pic x.
01   TriMatch            pic 9.
01   EndOfFile           pic s9(9) comp value external rmseof.
Procedure Division.
declaratives.
DvFaIn section.
    use after standard exception procedure on FaIn.
end declaratives.
themain section.
begin-triangle.
open input FaIn
```

```
read FaIn into WaIn
evaluate true
  when rmssts of FaIn = EndOfFile
    move 'y' to WaEof
  when rmssts ofFaIn > EndOfFile
    move 'n' to WaEof
  when rmssts of FaIn < EndOfFile
    move 'n' to WaEof
end-evaluate.
iter1.
evaluate true
  when WaEof < 'y'
    continue
  when WaEof ='y'
    go end-iter1
  when WaEof > 'y'
    continue
end-evaluate
evaluate true
  when I + J > K
    evaluate true
      when J + K > I
        evaluate true
          when K + I > J
            move 0 to TriMatch
            evaluate true
              when I = J
                compute TriMatch = TriMatch + 1
            end-evaluate
            evaluate true
              when J = K
                compute TriMatch = TriMatch + 1
            end-evaluate
            evaluate true
              when K = I
                compute TriMatch = TriMatch + 1
            end-evaluate
            evaluate true
              when TriMatch = 0 display 'Scalene'
              when TriMatch = 1 display 'Isosceles'
              when TriMatch = 3 display 'Equilateral'
              when TriMatch = 2 display 'Error'
              when TriMatch > 3 display 'Error'
            end-evaluate
```

```
        when K + I <= J
            display 'Not a Triangle'
        end-evaluate
      when J + K <= I
        display 'Not a Triangle'
    end-evaluate
  when I + J <= K
    display 'Not a Triangle'
end-evaluate
read FaIn into WaIn
evaluate true
  when rmssts of FaIn = EndOfFile
    move 'y' to WaEof
  when rmssts of FaIn > EndOfFile
    continue
  when rmssts of FaIn < EndOfFile
    continue
end-evaluate
go iter1.
end-iter1.
close FaIn
stop run.
end program triangle.
```

Consider a path through the above program with the following path condition:

$$I@1 + J@1 > K@1 \wedge J@1 + K@1 > I@1 \wedge K@1 + I@1 > J@1 \wedge I@1 = J@1 \wedge$$
$$J@1 = K@1 \wedge K@1 = I@1 \wedge I@2 + J@2 > K@2 \wedge J@2 + K@2 > I@2 \wedge$$
$$\neg K@2 + I@2 > J@2$$

This path reads two records, the string 'Equilateral' is displayed after the first, 'Not a Triangle' after the second. (Note that I@1 represents the first value read into I, I@2 the second value etc.)

This path condition together with the variable declarations can be expressed as the following linear programming problem.

Objective function	None

General constraints	$0 <= I@1 <= 9$
	$0 \leq J@1 \leq 9$
	$0 \leq K@1 \leq 9$
	$0 \leq I@2 \leq 9$
	$0 \leq J@2 \leq 9$
	$0 \leq K@2 \leq 9$

Specific constraints	$+1.0E - 21 \leq I@1 + J@1 - K@1 \leq +1.0E + 21$

$$+1.0E - 21 \leq J@1 + K@1 - I@1 \leq +1.0E + 21$$
$$+1.0E - 21 \leq K@1 + I@1 - J@1 \leq +1.0E + 21$$
$$0 \leq I@1 - J@1 \leq 0$$
$$0 \leq J@1 - K@1 \leq 0$$
$$0 \leq K@1 - I@1 \leq 0$$
$$+1.0E - 21 \leq I@2 + J@2 - K@2 \leq +1.0E + 21$$
$$+1.0E - 21 \leq J@2 + K@2 - I@2 \leq +1.0E + 21$$
$$-1.0E + 21 \leq K@2 + I@2 - J@2v0$$

The initial point which is thought to be feasible can be assumed to be values of zero for each variable.

The output is a feasible solution, for example:

$$I@1 = 1 \wedge J@1 = 1 \wedge K@1 = 1 \wedge I@2 = 0 \wedge J@2 = 1 \wedge K@2 = 0.$$

Because a feasible point is identified there are no contradictory constraints, the path is therefore feasible. The values that represent the feasible point can be used as a test case which will cause execution of the identified path.

6.4.5 Section summary

COBOL programs rarely, if ever, contain non-linear path conditions so it is appropriate to use a linear programming routine to assess path feasibility. SYM-BOL uses the NAG-library linear optimizer E04MBF. An advantage of this optimizer is that it can be used to return the first feasible solution rather than an optimal solution, thus reducing the time to assess feasibility. The use of optimizers is not in itself new. What is new is their application to COBOL programs which bring two problems not previously described in the literature.

The first problem is the existence of alphanumeric literals (string constants) on the path condition. Linear programming optimizers require numerics not strings. The solution adopted in SYM-BOL requires the substitution of numeric tokens in place of the alphanumeric literals in such a way that the sort sequence of the original strings is reflected in the sequence of the numeric tokens.

The second problem concerns record and group data items. Consider the following record declarations.

```
01   A1.
     03   A2 pic x.
     03   A3 pic x.
01   B1.
     03   B2 pic x.
     03   B3 pic x.
```

A predicate containing the variable $A1$, implicitly references the variables

$A2$ and $A3$. For example, the predicate $A1 = B1$ contains the two implied predicates $A2 = B2$ and $A3 = B3$. Where a path condition contains the predicates $A1 = B1$ and $A2 > B2$ then the implied predicates are significant. It is only by considering the implied predicates that the path infeasibility, caused by $A2 = B2$ and $A2 > B2$, will be identified. A symbolic execution testing system must, therefore, automatically include all implied predicates or, alternatively, process all variables as a series of characters. The second of these two approaches is discussed in the next chapter.

There is a third problem which concerns acceptable classes of constraints. Linear programming optimizers cannot process constraints of the form $A \neq B$, only constraints of the form $A <= B$ and $A >= B$ are generally acceptable to such routines. This problem is not described in the literature. Branches with such constraints are replaced by two branches $A < B$, down one branch, and $A > B$ down the other. Not only does this solution overcome the problematic branch predicate but it can also be used to force improved boundary testing. For example, consider $a = b$ where a and b are unsigned numerics This statement should be tested with the cases $a = b \wedge a + 1 = b$ and $a - 1 = b$.

To achieve good boundary testing the transformation incorporated in the first stage translation into standard form creates the branches $a = b \wedge a > b$ and $a < b$. By minimizing the objective function, $a + b$, for each branch the following three sets of values for a and b will be produced: 0,0; 0,1 and 1,0. These values represent good boundary tests.

The literature does not discuss the problems of assessing the feasibility of path conditions containing alphanumeric literals, implicit constraints created by group items and records and constraints of the form $A \neq B$. None of the earlier systems cater for these situations. SYM-BOL is, thus, novel in catering for all of them.

CHAPTER 7

Conclusions

7.1 Introduction

This chapter summarises the achievements which were detailed in the previous chapters and outlines further work that should be carried out in the area of symbolic execution.

7.2 Problems of applying symbolic execution

There are a number of general problems facing those who want to apply symbolic application. These include:

- ambiguous array references;
- path explosion when symbolically executing into called sub-programs;
- loop processing.

There are also a number of problems more specific to the application of symbolic execution to COBOL. These include:

- the size of the language, in particular a large variety of branching constructs;
- the fact that several files of many records constitute a single test case for a path;
- the fact that a mixture of interactive user input and reading of file data often occurs in a single test case;
- the presence of strings in predicates to be solved when assessing path feasibility;
- the redefinition of record structures and reference modification;
- the preponderance of string processing using string handling verbs.

The SYM-BOL system caters for most of these problems. Exceptions are redefinition, reference modification and the string handling verbs.

7.2.1 Large construct variety in COBOL

The large size of the language has been overcome by defining a core set of COBOL features. A set of standard forms has been established, one for each of: assignment; branching; and arithmetic calculations. By constructing a translator as the first part of the SYM-BOL system, a COBOL program using a wide range of COBOL features is transformed into an equivalent COBOL program containing only the standard forms.

The symbolic execution component of SYM-BOL processes only the standard forms. This has two main benefits. First, development of the SYM-BOL system could be carried out without concern for all the features of COBOL yet the system would process a working COBOL program. More COBOL features can be processed by adding translation functions to the first stage translator without the need to change the symbolic executor. Second, future changes to COBOL will require additions and changes only to the first-stage translator unless there are fundamental changes to the language. This is unlikely as COBOL has a long history of slow (perhaps too slow) change and most old features are supported in later language standards.

Other systems make a single step translation into intermediate form. In the event of the addition of a new language construct or a modification to an existing language feature the whole translation software will be subject to modification.

7.2.2 Path selection

Both automatic and user path selection mechanisms are included in the SYM-BOL system. The automatic selector uses a combination of current variable expressions, branch coverage and variable domain coverage criteria to choose the next branch to be added to the path. The aim of the strategy is to achieve selection of feasible paths, coverage of each branch and the production of paths that cover large variable domains.

Both automatic and user path selectors utilize the benefits of undertaking path selection and symbolic execution together. The result is avoidance of selection of infeasible paths caused by branch predicates being infeasible based upon their current expressions.

Immediate feasibility checking of the path condition once a branch has been added also prevents the creation of infeasible paths, as an alternative branch can be selected as soon as the path condition becomes infeasible. This co-ordinated approach to path selection and symbolic execution is a significant advance on many of the earlier systems which treated the two processes separately one after the other. As a result, the creation of infeasible paths is reduced.

7.2.3 Using linear programming for feasibility checking

Fortunately, COBOL programs rarely exhibit non-linear predicates; thus linear programming optimizers are appropriate for feasibility checking. Predicates containing string constants are a problem as a string cannot be passed to a numeric optimizer. This has been overcome by replacing string constants by numeric tokens. The substitution has only one rule: the original sort sequence of all such substituted strings must be maintained. This transformation is sufficient to allow the successful use of a linear optimizer for feasibility checking. Previous research has not identified strings as a problem for feasibility checking using linear optimizers.

7.3 Practicality of a COBOL symbolic execution testing system

The SYM-BOL system is not a complete system exhibiting all the desired features. Nevertheless, it is at such a stage of development that it provides all the expected features of symbolic execution such as:

- creating a path condition for a path;
- creating expressions for output variables;
- determining path feasibility;
- creating test data for a path;
- verifying simple assertions.

The system also includes some new features summarized earlier in this chapter, it:

- symbolically executes COBOL programs;
- assesses feasibility of path conditions containing strings;
- co-ordinates path selection and symbolic execution so reducing the number of infeasible paths generated;
- displays branch coverage at each branch selection;
- maintains details of inter-relationships of records in files.

There are some problems and impractical aspects of a COBOL symbolic execution testing system. The main ones are:

- the presence of constructs of a high level of abstraction such as sort and inspect;
- the presence of string handling facilities making the maintenance of variable expressions rather cumbersome.

These are not insurmountable. A more pertinent question is whether the means of overcoming the impracticalities outweigh the benefits to be gained. The maintenance of the relationship between records in different files is at the heart of testing commercial data processing software.

SYM-BOL keeps track of these aspects and while, in practice, it is not a trivial matter it is not conceptually difficult. The benefit is the documentation of the testing activity which is a valuable benefit not outweighed by the need to maintain the information. The major weaknesses of SYM-BOL are primarily those of symbolic execution in general, rather than of symbolic execution applied to COBOL. Symbolic execution is, in some ways, more useful when applied to COBOL programs because it can keep track of the error prone task of record interrelationships, a feature not required by other classes of software.

7.4 Strengths of the SYM-BOL system

Predicates containing string constants cannot normally be passed to a numeric optimizer as part of a system of constraints representing the path condition. An effective technique has been devised to allow substitution of these string constants with numeric tokens.

Path generation and symbolic execution are undertaken together. This allows the intermediate results from the symbolic execution to help in path selection and reduces the risk of selecting infeasible paths.

During path selection branch coverage is maintained allowing selection of uncovered branches in preference to already covered branches.

Commercial data processing software exhibits multiple input and output files. The system maintains symbolic values for each field in each record in each input file and expressions for each field in each record in each output file.

In addition to generating feasible path conditions the system also devises test data to cause execution of the path. This is organised into data files such that the program under test can simply be executed without the need for user intervention to create the test files.

7.5 Weaknesses of the SYM-BOL system

In its current prototype form SYM-BOL exhibits a number of weaknesses.

First, the number of COBOL constructs that may be used in the source program is restricted. Some of the accepted constructs are accepted only in limited forms. It is however debatable as to whether this is a weakness of the SYM-BOL system or of the COBOL language itself.

Second, validation of the input source program for non-acceptable constructs and the quality of diagnostic messages is weak.

Third, the system does not record the state of the path condition and variables at each branch point. This is necessary when the system is to provide replay and retrace facilities such as those provided by EXDAMS [Bal69]. However, this was not established as a fundamental requirement of the system and it would not be a difficult omission to rectify.

Fourth, the analysis of the intermediate form for path selection and symbolic execution is based on the transformed 'source' program rather than the original source program. While this has some advantages, it also means that the user is presented with information that is not necessarily congruent with the source program submitted to the system. This would not be a problem if the information was cross-referenced to the original source program but at present no cross-referencing is undertaken.

Fifth, the user interface is rather crude, driven from a menu in teletype mode, with, as a result, poor screen handling.

Finally, perhaps COBOL is not regarded as one of the best languages for building software tools. However, many of the alternatives had major weaknesses such as not easily supporting the implementation of data hiding within modules. COBOL posed no such problems and is quite suitable for much of the housekeeping processing that is required.

7.6 Symbolic execution and the general features of programming languages

When assessing the usefulness of a technique it is helpful to consider it in terms of the general features of programming languages rather than to limit the discussion to one particular language. The final sections of this book briefly consider the usefulness of symbolic execution when applied to programs in general and also the effectiveness of the SYM-BOL system for COBOL programs.

7.6.1 Module calls

A module call is any invocation of out-of-line code. At the point where control is passed to the out-of-line code there is a choice over whether to use macro-expansion or the lemma approach. This does not cause a difficulty, but merely presents a choice of approaches. By considering the position of the variable declarations for variables used in both the calling program and the called routine a spectrum of module calls can be identified ranging from the global-only to the parameter-only.

The simplest module call may be termed a 'global-only call'. Here, the variables declared in the calling program are the only variables used in the module i.e. only global variables are in use. Symbolic execution in general and also the SYM-BOL system can sensibly deal with these routines, the path condition and variable expressions are updated in the usual way.

The next module call can be described as the 'parameterless call'. Here data is passed between called and calling programs by using global variables, but local variables may also be in use within the module. When the same identifier is used for both local and global variables, symbolic execution must be careful to modify only expressions for local variables. Other than this, the use of local variables does not cause a complication for symbolic execution. The SYM-BOL system does not cater for this form of module call.

The worst module to execute symbolically is what can be termed the 'parameter-global' call. This type of call passes parameters but also produces side effects in global variables. As a result it suffers the same difficulty as the parameterless call but in addition some results are returned by a parameter mechanism. Care must be taken to avoid amending both local and parameter expressions for variables with the same identifier in both module and calling program. Symbolic execution can cope with this type of module but the SYM- BOL system has not been designed to cater for such module calls.

The neatest module to execute symbolically is the parameter-only module call. Here, the source data received from and the results returned to the calling program are passed only by parameter passing mechanisms. Symbolic execution of the module can be undertaken independently of or in concert with the calling modules. The SYM-BOL system has been designed to process such module calls.

Parameter passing

When a module is invoked the actual parameters provided in the calling program must be supplied to the formal parameters in the module. Barron [Bar77] identifies three main means of passing parameters:

- call by value;
- call by reference;
- call by name.

Pratt [Pra84] has identified more categories of parameter passing, but these do not need any additional techniques above those required by the three mechanisms listed above.

A 'call by value' simply supplies a copy of the value in the actual parameter to the formal parameter. Symbolic execution processes this call by simply copying the expression for the actual parameter to the expression for the formal parameter. This has been implemented in SYM-BOL.

A 'call by reference' supplies a reference (or address) of the actual parameter to the formal parameter. Any change to the formal parameter is a change to the actual parameter as the actual and formal parameter identifiers are in effect synonyms for the same storage location. Symbolic execution can handle this in two ways.

First, it can treat the call in much the same way as for call by value, i.e. the expression for the actual parameter is copied to the expression for the formal parameter. In addition the evaluation of the actual parameter is pushed onto a call stack. Immediately on return of control to the calling program the actual parameter is popped from the stack and the expression for the formal parameter is copied to the expression of the actual parameter.

Second, the actual and formal parameters can be treated as though they were synonyms. Whenever a change is made to a formal parameter it is the expression for the actual parameter which is modified.

As both of these approaches mirror established means of implementing call by reference and their effect is equivalent there is no reason to choose one approach over the other. SYM-BOL is designed to handle call by reference by the second approach using the same mechanism that handles simple variable redefinition.

A 'call by name' defers the evaluation of actual parameters until they are used. It is the called module that determines when, if ever, they are evaluated. The effect is as though the actual parameter is substituted in place of every occurrence of the formal parameter in the called module before execution of the module commences.

Symbolic execution of call by name is achieved by passing the name of the parameter rather than by passing the expression that represents the current evaluation of the parameter name. During execution of the called module whenever a formal parameter is encountered it is substituted by the parameter name. Thereafter symbolic execution continues as usual.

A further means of parameter passing is 'call by value and pass back', alternatively known as 'call by value/result'. This is implemented in much the same way as 'call by value'. On invocation the contents of the actual parameters are copied into the formal parameters. On exit the contents of the formal parameters are copied back into the actual parameters. This appears to achieve the same results as 'call by reference' but the two methods are not semantically equivalent. Myers [Mye79] gives an example to demonstrate that the four means of parameter passing discussed above can yield four different results. When implementing a symbolic execution tool care must be taken to ensure that the semantic differences between the various parameter passing mechanisms are maintained.

In short there are three fundamental parameter passing mechanisms illustrated by the following:

call r using value $c(m)$ value passed 8
call r using reference $c(m)$ value passed $c(2)$
call r using name $c(m)$ value passed c(m)

All of these are easily symbolically executed in the normal way. The value '8' can be instantly included in an expression. The value $c(2)$ is replaced by its current expression which is then incorporated into in an expression. The value $c(m)$ undergoes two substitutions prior to inclusion in an expression. First, substitute m by its current expression. Second, substitute the whole of the resulting expression by its current expression. Now it is ready for final inclusion in an expression. All of these steps are part of general symbolic execution and so none of the three parameter passing mechanisms poses a difficulty for symbolic execution.

Recursion

The only difference between a recursive call and an ordinary call is that the recursive call creates a second activation of the subprogram during the lifetime of the first activation [Pra84]. Compilers cope with this difference by the use of a central stack to store the activation records. Symbolic execution can cope with recursion in much the same way. When a recursive call is made the current activation containing the expressions for all variables is pushed onto the central stack. Parameter passing is handled in the usual way as described in the previous section. On exit form the recursively called module the central stack is popped and the activation yielded replaces the current activation.

Recursion is not supported by COBOL and is, therefore not a feature of SYM- BOL.

Parallelism

There are two approaches to executing symbolically concurrent modules: the interleaving and the isolation approaches [Dil88].

The interleaving approach merely combines the concurrent modules to form a larger sequential module. This suffers from a combinatorial explosion of paths which grows exponentially with the number of modules. In addition there are difficulties in demonstrating that the form of interleaving chosen does not overlook a potential behaviour.

The isolation approach symbolically executes the concurrent modules independently, then attempts to show that the concurrent modules cooperate and do not suffer from deadlock. Entry assertions for a module specify the constraints on global constants i.e. the nature of the environment. Exit assertions specify the relationship between a module's local variables on termination. Global invariants specify the relationship between variables in different modules. Path conditions are generated for each module to demonstrate its local correctness. Path conditions used in demonstrating local correctness together with global invariants on the local paths are combined to produce verification conditions. If the verification conditions are feasible, then the global invariants are upheld and cooperation between parallel modules is demonstrated.

Demonstrating the absence of deadlock requires the creation of an assertion that countenances deadlock. Dillon [Dil88] lists three such syntactic features. These can be used to generate a blocking assertion. If a path containing a blocking assertion is not contradictory then it is prey to deadlock.

Concurrent execution of modules is not provided in COBOL and so this feature is not provided in SYM-BOL.

7.6.2 Data Structuring

Discussion so far in this section has concentrated on symbolic execution's ability to cater for the features of procedural decomposition provided by programming languages. Data structuring also provides problems worthy of consideration. Symbolic execution of atomic data items is reasonably straightforward but compound data items, which are aggregates of simple items, require more sophisticated handling. Sometimes, the aggregates are manipulated as a whole, on other occasions reference to the individual components is required.

Barron [Bar77] classifies data aggregates into arrays and structures. Arrays are aggregates in which the components are identified by their position within he aggregate. Structures are aggregates in which the components are identified by name. This classification appears to omit a category for files and dynamic data structures which make use of pointers. A further category, 'sequence', can also be defined which are aggregates in which the components are not identified but are retrieved simply in the order of storage.

Unfortunately, this still leaves sets unclassified. The fact that a set contains unordered items conflicts with the members of the sequence class where order is important. Sets therefore constitute a class of their own. and we will define them as are aggregates in which the components are not identified and are not retrieved by use of the order of storage.

Arrays

Arrays, strings and direct access files can all be placed in Barron's array class. The well known problem of symbolic execution of arrays is the ambiguous array reference. Here, the index is dependent on one or more input variables. As a result it is not resolved which element is to be the destination for an assignment or which element is to be compared in a condition test.

Strings (arrays of characters) can be processed in two ways. First, they can be processed as a whole and as such can be symbolically executed provided the techniques such as those described in this book are employed to deal with difficulties faced in feasibility checking. Second, strings can be processed as though they are an array of characters. In this situation their symbolic execution is subject to the same difficulties as arrays in general.

Records held within direct access files, like elements within arrays and characters within strings, are identified by their position within the file. The key field may be subjected to a hash function to yield the location within the file of the desired record but this merely constitutes a 'coded' identification by position. Again, as with arrays, if during symbolic execution the expression for the desired key is dependent on input variables then ambiguous references result.

Overall, Barron's array class is problematic for symbolic execution for just the reason that constitutes the rule of membership of the class. Identification by position, cannot easily be handled when the position is dependent upon input variables.

Structures

Many languages use the term 'record' to refer to structures. Here component items are identified by name. Symbolic execution has no problem in performing the basic processing of items identified by name. The only difficulty that arises is in feasibility checking.

A record structure comprises several elementary items. Each item may be the subject of a component constraint on a path condition. The whole record may also be the subject of one or more constraints. There is a risk that conflicting constraints may go undetected because the relationship between a whole record and its component items is not apparent to the feasibility checker. This can be overcome by breaking down constraints containing whole records into several constraints on its components. Any contradictions will now be apparent during feasibility checking.

Sequences

This classification includes sequential files and dynamic data structures which make use of pointers. The main feature of this class is that items are retrieved simply in the order of storage. The problem for symbolic execution is to maintain information about the sequence of the items.

Sequential files can be handled quite simply. Each time a record is read a position counter is incremented. Each symbolic value introduced as result of this read is tagged with the position counter. Account must be taken of the position counter tag when generating files of test cases ready for execution in order to achieve the correct ordering of records in the file.

When a file is opened symbolic execution notes the opening and the access mode. Should a read be attempted on an unopened file or on a file opened only for output, symbolic execution will detect this. Similarly, symbolic execution will detect attempts to write to unopened files or files opened only for input. The end of file test can also be handled by symbolic execution by creating a data item to indicate whether the file is open or closed.

The pointer used in maintaining dynamic data structures is simply an address for the storage location of the item. Any list or sequence that is implemented using pointers can also be implemented using a static mechanism such as an array and replacing the pointer by an integer subscript.

Symbolic execution can make use of this alternative implementation by using it as model for dynamic sequences. A relative pointer (subscript) can be maintained based on the starting position of the sequence. Symbolic execution merely increments the relative position each time progression to the next item takes place. The expression for the pointer is used only to indicate the position in the sequence for the purpose of generation of test data. As the pointer value is inaccessible within the program no information is lost by adopting this approach.

The only difficulty with the relative-position-pointer approach occurs when items are deleted from the sequence. There appears to be two possible approaches. First, the whole set of pointer expressions must be appropriately adjusted each time a deletion takes place. Second, the set of pointer expressions are left intact and the details of the deletion noted. Immediately prior to the generation of test data or feasibility assessment the pointer expressions must be adjusted. Both of these approaches are unwieldy for large sequences. However, it is unlikely that symbolic execution would be used in the creation of large sequences for validation and verification purposes so in practice this is unlikely to pose a significant problem.

Sets

There are two categories of operation on a set. First, a set can be tested for emptiness or to determine whether an item is a member of the set. Second, the contents of a set can be modified by: insert, delete, union, intersection and difference operations.

When symbolic execution makes a membership test on a set the two possibilities of true and false can be instantly assessed by searching the list of values (expressions) that constitute the list. If a matching expression is found then the predicate is true and the constraint can be ignored. If no matching expression is found then it either indicates that the search argument is not in the set or that the matching expression is not in a recognizable form or that the match cannot be resolved because of the presence of symbolic values for input variables. In this case the expression being sought is to be conjoined to the path condition. This is problematic because no straightforward constraint(s) can be found to represent such a predicate when the set may contain anything other than a limited number of values.

When symbolic execution encounters an empty test on a set the truth can be resolved simply so long as the number of items in the set has been maintained. In essence this requires the symbolic executor to simulate the implementation of the set constructs. This is similar to the methods required for handling other high-level constructs.

A list of the symbolic expressions that constitute the items in the set can be maintained by the symbolic executor. There is no difficulty in symbolically executing operations that require only the addition of new items so insert and union can be handled successfully. But, again as with testing for set membership, recognition of the expression that represents an item to be deleted is a problem. Thus delete, intersection and difference cannot be guaranteed to be symbolically executed correctly.

7.7 Concluding remarks

There are two important questions to be answered at this stage. First, can symbolic execution be usefully applied to programming languages in general? Second, can symbolic execution be applied to commercial data processing software in particular to COBOL programs?

All the elementary features of programming languages can be handled by symbolic execution. Of the more sophisticated decompositional features many can be handled in a straightforward manner. The more advanced features of module calling such as call by name, recursion and parallelism can be handled with the introduction of additional supporting mechanisms not developed when the technique was first mooted some 15 or so years ago.

The one stumbling block for symbolic execution is the array. However, the adoption of the viewpoint that sees determining a value for an ambiguous array reference as a matter for path selection allows the technique to progress and provide useful results which are otherwise unobtainable.

Whether symbolic execution can be applied to commercial data processing software and in particular to COBOL programs requires the answer to address the following:

- general problems of symbolic execution that apply to COBOL programs;
- specific problems that COBOL brings to symbolic execution;
- unsurmounted problems and their level of detraction from the usefulness of the technique.

The literature describes two main problems facing the general application of symbolic execution. These are ambiguous array references and path selection, especially loops and module calls. Earlier it was suggested that ambiguous array references can be handled as another aspect of path selection. By choosing a particular index value a virtual path is selected. This could be accomplished by inserting an n-way branch, where n is the number of elements in the array, into the program at the point where an ambiguous array reference occurs. Resolving ambiguous array references in practice then becomes a matter of path selection. This view reduces all the general problems to one of path selection.

The notion of path selection as a problem for symbolic execution has stood for some time and needs challenging. Path selection is a part of the structural approach to testing software. Symbolic execution is a technique that creates expressions for variables and isolates the conditions that must be true to cause execution of a particular path. These results are useful when testing software. The goal is to carefully test the software not merely to undertake symbolic execution for its own sake. Whether symbolic execution is used or not, path selection is fundamental to the structural approach to testing. A major problem of path selection is the avoidance of infeasible paths. Symbolic execution can be used to assess path feasibility. Symbolic execution may more properly be viewed as a technique for aiding path selection rather than the more usual view that path selection is a hindrance to symbolic execution.

The specific problems that COBOL brings to symbolic execution revolve around the high level of abstraction of many COBOL constructs and the low level of data referencing possible in COBOL. Assignments of the form:

move a to b

are of a low level of abstraction when compared to the following:

inspect a tallying in b for all c

Data references may be partitioned into two types. Consider the following data declarations and three data references:

a pic $x(10)$.
b pic $x(5)$ occurs 10.

1   a
2    $a(5:7)$
3    $b(6)$

The first reference refers to all of the characters assigned to the identifier a. Lines 2 and 3 refer to a subset of the characters assigned to identifiers a and b, the fifth, sixth and seventh characters of a and the sixth element of b respectively.

7.7.1 High level constructs

At first sight there seems to be little to be gained from substituting high level constructs with more detailed equivalent code before symbolic execution. This amounts to macro-expansion of functions that are known to be correct which could alternatively be treated as an I/O boundary. On the other hand, the code that is substituted has a set of paths which, if fully explored, would give rise to a set of test cases which would test in some detail the output possibilities of the high level construct. In the same way that symbolic execution systems should give the user a choice over whether to employ macro expansion or to use an I/O boundary for module calls, the same facility may also be provided for higher level constructs. It is not necessarily the module or the construct that is being assessed rather it is the use of the module or construct within the program that is on trial. Not only is this approach useful for COBOL but it also has application in the testing of higher level languages. The tester may be prompted to make choices about the nature of the data in a particular test case. This can be achieved using construct standard forms and path selection.

7.7.2 Low level data referencing

The notion of the identifier as the lowest level data reference is inadequate to cater for string processing. By maintaining expressions for individual characters symbolic execution can cater for all features of COBOL programs. The use of data usages other than display, such as binary and computational, does not impact upon symbolic execution as the procedural part of the source program is unaffected by this hidden data representation.

7.8 Conclusion

It is clear that symbolic execution can be applied to COBOL programs and used to verify simple assertions and generate files of test cases ready for execution. Further research is needed to establish whether the effort required to use such a COBOL tool might be better spent in using an alternative approach to software testing. The SYM-BOL prototype is a strong basis from which to undertake this research.

Appendix A

The SYM-BOL system uses a dialect of the COBOL programming language. The aim of this brief appendix is to describe the main features of this language. A typical program is shown below

```
Identification Division.
Program-Id. P9a.
Environment Division.
Data Division.
Working-Storage Section.
01 NiDetails.
    02 NiRate            pic 99v99.
01 TaxDetails.
    02 TaxFree           pic 9(4)v99.
    02 TaxRate           pic 99v9.
    02 taxable           pic 9(5)v99.
Linkage section.
01 InputParameters.
    02 gross             pic 9(5)v99.
    02 TaxCode           pic 9(4).
    02 NiClass           pic x.
    02 frequency         pic x.
        88 weekly        value 'w'.
        88 monthly       value 'm'.
01 OutputParameters.
    02 state   picx.
        88 err           value 'e'.
        88 no-error      value 'n'.
    02 tax               pic 9(4)v99.
    02 ni                pic 9(3)v99.

Procedure division using
InputParameters OutputParameters.

The-program.
    move 'n' to state.
```

* Set the national insurance rate
evaluate true
    when $NiClass =$ 'a'   move 0.05 to $ni - rate$
    when $NiClass =$ 'b'   move 0.10 to $ni - rate$
    when $NiClass =$ 'c'   move 0.15 to $ni - rate$
    when other   move 0.0 to $ni - rate$
                      move 'e' to *state*
                      display "ni class error"
end-evaluate

* set tax free
if *state* not $=$ 'e'
then
  if *monthly*
  then
    compute $TaxFree = TaxCode * 10/12$ end-compute
  end-if
  if *weekly*
  then
    compute $tax - free = tax - code * 10/52$ end-compute
  end-if
  if not *monthly* and not *weekly*
  then
    move 0 to $TaxFfree$
    move 'e' to *state*
    display 'error in pay period'
  end-if
end-if

* set tax rate
if *state* not$=$ 'e'
then
  compute $taxable = gross - TaxFree$ end-compute
  if $taxable < 10000$
  then
    move 0.3 to *tax-rate*
  else
    if $taxable < 20000$
    then
      move 0.4 to $tax - rate$
    else
      move 0.5 to $tax - rate$
    end-if
  end-if

```
* calculate deductions
    compute ni = NiRate * gross end-compute
    compute tax = TaxRate * taxable end-compute
end-if

exit program.
end program P9a.
```

The program consists of a number of divisions. The Identification Division identifies the program. The Environment Division identifies the hardware environment in which the program will execute. In the program above this is left blank and a system default used. The Data Division defines the format of files used in the program, together with any non-file variables. These latter variables are defined in a section known as the Working Storage Section. A program can be treated as a subroutine and the parameters used are defined in a section known as the Linkage Section. Records are defined by prefacing them with a number, Each level of a record is subdivided into fields by increasing this number and into sub-fields by further increasing this number. So, for example, the record $TaxDetails$ is decomposed into three fields $TaxFree$, $TaxRate$ and $taxable$. The format of individual fields is defined using the keyword *pic*. For example $TaxCode$ is defined as pic 9(4). This specifies that this variable will contain four digits.

The final division of a COBOL program is known as the Procedure Division. The procedure division of the program above is self explanatory: comments are introduced by means of *, **if** statements are delimited by if and end-if and the keyword **move** indicates that a value has been moved to a variable.

The only important procedural facility not contained in the example program is the execution of loops. These are introduced by means of the perform statement. An example is shown below:

```
perform until x = y
code
end-perform
```

This executes the code in its body until the variables x and y are equal.

References

[Alj79] M.M. Al-Jarrah and I.S. Torsun (1979) An empirical analysis of COBOL programs. *Software Practice and Experience*, 9:341–379.

[And79] D. Andrews (1979) Using executable assertions for testing and fault tolerance. In *Proceedings of the International Conference on Fault-Tolerant Computing.*

[Asi79] P. Asirelli, P. Degano, G. Levi, *et al.* (1979) A flexible environment for program development based on a symbolic interpreter. In *Proceedings of the Fourth International Conference on Software Engineering*, pages 251–263.

[Bal69] R. M. Balzer (1969) EXDAMS extendable debugging and monitoring system. In *Proceedings of the Spring AFIPS joint conference*, pages 567–580.

[Bar77] D. W. Barron (1977) *An Introduction to the Study of Programming Languages.* Cambridge University Press.

[Bas87] V.R. Basili (1987) Comparing the effectiveness of testing strategies. *IEEE Transactions on Software Engineering*, 13(12):1278—96.

[Baz82] F. Bazzichi and I. Spadafora (1982) An automatic generator for compiler testing. *IEEE Transactions on Software Engineering*, 8(4):343–53.

[Bic79] J. Bicevskis, J. Borzovs, U. Straujums, A. Zarins, and E.F. Miller (1979) SMOTL–a system to construct samples for data processing program debugging. *IEEE Transactions on Software Engineering*, 5(1):60–66.

[Boy75] R.S. Boyer, B. Elpas, and K.N. Levit (1975) SELECT – a formal system for testing and debugging programs by symbolic execution. In *Proceedings of the International Conference on Reliable Software*, pages 234–44, 1975.

[Bud78] T.A. Budd and R.J. Lipton (1978) Mutation analysis of decision table programs. In *Proceedings of the Conference on Information Science and Systems*, pages 346–79.

[Bud80] T.A. Budd, R.A. Demillo, R.J. Lipton, and F.G. Sayward (1980) Theoretical and empirical studies on using program mutation to test the functional correctness of programs. In *Proceedings of the seventh ACM Symposium on the Principles of Programming languages*, pages 220–22.

[Car86] B.A. Carre, I.M. O'Neill, D.L. Clutterbuck, and C.W. Debney (1986) SPADE—the southampton program analysis and development environment. In I. Sommerville, editor, *Software Engineering Environments*. Peter Peregrinus.

[Cha79] J. Chan (1979) *Program Debugging Methodology.* PhD thesis, Leicester Polytechnic.

[Che79] T. E. Cheatham, G.H. Holloway, and Townley J.A (1979) Symbolic evaluation and the analysis of programs. *IEEE Transactions on Software Engineering*, 5(5):402–417.

[Cla76a] L.A. Clarke (1976) A program testing system. In *Proceedings ACM Conference*, pages 488–491.

[Cla76b] L.A. Clarke (1976) A system to generate test data and symbolically execute programs. *IEEE Transactions on Software Engineering*, 2(3):215–22.

[Cla81] L.A. Clarke and D.J. Richardson (1981) Symbolic evaluation methods - implementations and applications. In B. Chandraeskaran and S Radicchi, editors, *Computer Program Testing*. North-Holland.

[Cla83] L.A. Clarke and D.J. Richardson (1983) The application of error-sensitive testing strategies to debugging. *SIGPLAN Notices*, 18(8):45–52.

[Cla85] L.A. Clarke and D.J. Richardson (1985) Applications of symbolic evaluation. *Journal of Systems and Software*, 5(1):15–35.

[Coe90] A. Coen-Parisi and F. De Paoli (1990) SYMBAD: a symbolic executor of sequential ada programs. In *Proceedings SafeComp 90*, pages 105–111.

[Coo76] D.W. Cooper. Adaptive testing (1976) In *Proceedings of the Second International Conference on Software Engineering*, pages 223–26.

[Dem79] R.A. Demillo, R.J. Lipton, and Perlis A.J. (1979) Social processes and proofs of theorems and programs. *Communications of the ACM*, 22(5):271–80.

[Dem81] T. De Marco (1981) *Structured Analysis and System Specification*. Yourdon Press.

[Dil88] L. K. Dillon (1988) Symbolic execution-based verification of Ada tasking programs. In *Proceedings of 3rd International IEEE Conference on Ada applications and environments*, pages 3–13.

[Dur81] J.W. Duran and S.C Ntafos (1981) A report on random testing. In *Proceedings of the Fifth International Conference on Software Engineering*, pages 179–183, 1981.

[Dur84] J.W. Duran and S.C. Ntafos (1984) An evaluation of random testing. *IEEE Transactions on Software Engineering*, 10(4):438–44.

[Elp72] B. Elpas, K.N. Levitt, R.J. Waldinger, and A. Waksman (1972) An assessment of techniques for proving program correctness. *Computing Surveys*, 4(2):97–14.

[Fis77] K. F. Fischer (1977) A test case selection method for the validation of software maintenance modification. In *Proceedings COMPSAC 77*, pages 421–426.

[Flo67] R.W. Floyd (1967) Assigning meaning to programs. In *Proceedings of Symposium in Applied Mathematics*, pages 19–32.

[Goo75] J.B. Goodenough and S.L. Gehart (1975) Towards a theory of test data selection. *IEEE Transactions on Software Engineering*, 1(2):156–73.

[Han70] K.V. Handford (1970) Automatic generation of test cases. *IBM Systems Journal*, 9(4):242–57.

[Han76] S.L. Hantler and J.C. King (1976) An introduction to proving the correctness of programs. *Computing Surveys*, 18(3):331–53.

[Har90] J. Hartmann and D.J. Robson (1990) Techniques for selective revalidation. *IEEE Software*, 7(1):31–36.

[Hay87] I. Hayes (1987) *Specification Case Studies*. Prentice-Hall.

[Hed81] D. Hedley (1981) *Automatic test data generation and related topics*. PhD thesis, Department of Computational Science, Liverpool University.

[Hek85] S. Hekmatpour and D. C. Ince (1985) *Software Prototyping, Formal Methods and VDM*. Addison-Wesley.

[Hen76] M.A. Hennell, M.R. Woodward, and D. Hedley (1976) On program analysis. *Information Processing Letters*, 5(5):136–140.

[Hen83] M.A. Hennell, D. Hedley, and I.J. Riddell (1983) The LDRA software testbeds: their roles and capabilities. In *Proceedings of the IEEE Software Fair 83 Conference.*

[Hoa69] C.A.R. Hoare (1969) An axiomatic basis for computer programming. *Communications of the ACM*, 12:576–580.

[How77] W.E. Howden (1977) Symbolic testing and the DISSECT symbolic evaluation system. *IEEE Transactions on Software Engineering*, 3(4):266–278.

[How78a] W.E. Howden (1978) DISSECT - a symbolic evaluation and program testing system. *IEEE Transactions on Software Engineering*, 3(4):266–278.

[How78b] W.E. Howden (1978) An evaluation of the effectiveness of symbolic testing. *Software Practice and Experience*, 8:381–97.

[How81] W. Howden (1981) Errors, design properties and functional program tests. In B. Chandrasekaran and S. Radicchi, editors, *Computer Program Testing.*

[Inc85] D.C. Ince (1985) The automatic generation of test data. *Computer Journal*, 30(1):63–69.

[Jac75] M. Jackson (1975) *Principles of Program Design.* Academic Press.

[Jon86] C.B. Jones (1986) *Systematic Software Development using VDM.* Prentice-Hall.

[Kan93] C. Kaner, J. Falk, and H. Q. Nguyen (1993) *Testing Computer Software.* Van Nostrand Rheinhold.

[Kem85] Kemmerer R.A. and S.T. Eckman (1985) UNISEX — a UNIX-based symbolic executor for pascal. *Software Practice and Experience*, 15(5):439–458.

[Kin75] J.C. King (1975) A new approach to program testing. In *Proceedings International Confernce on Reliable Software*, pages 228–233.

[Kin76] J.C. King (1976) Symbolic execution and program testing. *Communications of the ACM*, 19(7):385–94.

[Kin81] J.C. King (1981) Program reduction using symbolic execution. *ACM SIGSOFT Software Engineering Notes*, 6(1):9–14.

[Lak76] I. Lakatos (1976) *Proofs and Refutations: the Logic of Mathematical Discovery.* Cambridge University Press.

[Loo88] P.S. Loo and W.K. Tsai (1988) Random testing revisited. *Information and Software Technology*, 30(7):402–417.

[Man73] Z. Manna, S. Ness, and J. Vuillemin (1973) Inductive methods for proving properties of programs. *Communications of the ACM*, 16(8):491–502.

[Mil63] J.C Miller and C.J. Maloney (1963) Systematic mistake analysis of digital computer programs. *Communications of the ACM*, 6(1):58–63.

[Mil74] E.F. Miller and M.R. Paige (1974) Automatic generation of software test-cases. In *Proceedings Eurocomp 74*, pages 1–12.

[Mye79] G.J. Myers (1979) *The Art of Software Testing.* John Wiley.

[One88] G. O'Neill (1988) Evaluation of the RTP Pascal-MALPAS IL translator. Report 128/88, National Physical Laboratory.

[One89] O'Neill I.M. and Clutterbuck D.L. (1989) Tool support for software proof. In *Proceedings of IEE Colloquium on the Application of Computer-aided Software Engineering Tools.*

[Ost76] L.J. Osterweil and L.D. Fosdick (1976) Some experience with DAVE—a FORTRAN program analyser. In *Proceedings AFIPS 76*, pages 909–15.

[Ost83] L.J. Osterweil (1983) TOOLPACK – an experimental software development environment research project. *IEEE Transactions on Software Engineering*, 9(6):673–85.

[Pai74] M.R. Paige (1974) The use of software probes in testing fortran programs. *IEEE Computer*, pages 40–47.

[Pay78] A.J. Payne (1978) A formalized technique for expressing compiler exercisers. *SIGPLAN Notices*, 13(1):59–69.

[Plo79] E. Ploedereder (1979) Pragmatic techniques for program analysis and verification. In *Proceedings of the Fourth International Conference on Software Engineering*, pages 63–72.

[Pra84] T. W. Pratt (1984) *Programming Languages—Design and Implementation*. Prentice-Hall.

[Ram74] C.V. Ramamoorthy and S.F. Ho (1974) FORTRAN automatic code evaluation system. Technical report, Electronics Research Lab, University of California.

[Ram76] C.V. Ramamoorthy, S.F. Ho, and W.J. Chen (1976) On the automated generation of program test data. *IEEE Transactions on Software Engineering*, 2(4):293–300.

[Ric81] D.J. Richardson and L.A Clarke (1981) A partition analysis method to increase program reliability. In *Proceedings Fifth International Conference on Software Engineering*, pages 244–53.

[Spe84] A. Spector and D. Gifford (1984) The space shuttle primary computer system. *Communications of the ACM*, 27(9):874–90.

[Tay83] R.N. Taylor (1983) An integrated verification and testing environment. *Software Practice and Experience*, 13:697–713.

[Van78] D. Van Tassel (1978) *Program Style, Design, Efficiency, Debugging and Testing*. Prentice-Hall.

[Vog80] V. Voges, L. Gmeiner, and A. Amschler (1980) SADAT — an automated testing tool. *IEEE Transactions on Software Engineering*, 6(3):286–290.

[Web87] J. T. Webb (1987) MALPAS —an automatic static analysis tool for software validation and verification. In *Proceedings of 1st International Conference on Reliability and Robustness of Engineering Software*, pages 67–75.

[Wei73] G.M. Weinberg (1973) *The Psychology of Computer Programming*. Van Nostrand Rheinhold.

[Wey80] E. J. Weyuker and T. J. Ostrand (1980) Theories of program testing and the application of revealing subdomains. *IEEE Transactions on Software Engineering*, 6(3):236–46.

[Wey82] E.J. Weyuker (1982) On testing non-testable programs. *Computer Journal*, 25(4):465–70.

[Whi80] L.J. White and E.I. Cohen (1980) A domain strategy for computer program testing. *IEEE Transactions on Software Engineering*, 6(3):247–257.

[Woo80] M.R. Woodward, D. Hedley, and M.A. Hennell (1980) Experience with path analysis and testing of programs. *IEEE Transactions on Software Engineering*, 6(6):278–85.

[Yau87] S.S. Yau and Z. Kishimoto (1987) A method for revalidating modified programs in the maintenance phase. In *Proceedings COMPSAC 1987*, pages 272–277.

Index

0-1 integer programming 59

Acceptance testing 2, 18
Ada 63, 70
Adaptive perturbation testing 17
Add verb 102, 116
Ambiguous array reference 68, 88, 137
Andrews D. 17
Anomaly analysis 11, 12, 15, 23
ANSI 73
ANSI standard FORTRAN 69
Arrays 137, 140
Assert statement 64
Assertion 11, 14, 15, 18, 32, 54, 63,
    68–70, 72, 77, 82, 91, 131, 136
Assertion checking 52, 54
Assertion violation 18
ATTEST 61, 64, 66–68, 80, 81, 87, 88,
    100, 114
Automated test generation 21
Automatic path selector 85
Automatic test data generator 21

Backward substitution 32, 42, 43, 45,
    46
Barron, D. W. 134, 137
Basili, V.R. 28, 29
Binary division 51
Black box approach 8
BNF 21
Boundary condition 20
Boundary testing 127
Boundary value analysis 26
Branch coverage 10, 130
Branch testing 23

Call by name 134, 135
Call by reference 134, 135

Call by value 134
Call by value/result 135
Call verb 103
Calling hierarchy 58
CASEGEN 21, 61, 64, 67–69, 80, 81,
    88, 100, 114
Cause effect graphing 16, 18
Cause-effect graph 19
Chan, J. 8
Chane, W. J. 49
Cheatham, T. E. 49
Clarke, L. A. 14, 32, 33, 51, 78
COBOL 5, 9, 33, 49, 50, 73, 80–83,
    85–89, 99, 101, 102, 110, 115, 126,
    129–131, 133, 140, 141
Code reading 26, 27
Cohen, E. I. 116
Coincidental correctness 59
Commercial data processing
    environment 110
Commercial data processing software
    115, 131, 132, 140
Compiler 21
Complete correctness 91
Compound condition 104
Computation change 56
Computation error 20, 21, 60
Compute verb 102, 116
Constraint 2, 66
Cooper D. W. , 17
Coverage metric 14, 21, 47, 72, 81

Data flow analysis 16
Data flow anomaly 16
DAVE 15
Debugging 32
Decision table 16, 18, 19
DeMillo, R.A. 15

Dillon, L. K. 136
Direct access file 137
Directed graph 13
DISSECT 61, 62
Divide verb 102
Domain and computation testing 19
Domain change 56
Domain coverage 130
Domain error 20, 60
Domain testing 20
Duran, J. W. 17
Dynamic analysis 11
Dynamic data structure 138
Dynamic symbolic evaluation 32
Dynamic-functional testing 16, 19

EFFIGY 61, 64, 65, 73, 77, 81, 87, 88,
    115
EL1 61
Equivalence class 17
Equivalence class partitioning 17, 26
Equivalence test 17
Evaluation of loops 46
EXDAMS 61, 62, 132
Executable assertion 18

FACES 15
Fault tolerant software 4
FDL 63
FDL Reader 63
Feasible path 46, 47, 88, 130
File handling 80
Fischer, K. F. 59
Flowgraph 13, 16, 64
Floyd, R. W. 14
Formal specification 3, 21
Formal verification 3
FORTRAN 16, 66, 67, 69, 81, 83, 87,
    110
FORTRAN test-bed 21, 61, 64, 69, 77,
    80, 87, 88, 100, 114
Forward expansion 32, 33, 36, 41, 42,
    46
Function 2
Functional requirement 1, 2
Functional specification 1
Functional structured testing 23

Functional testing 2, 7, 11, 26, 27
Functional testing strategy 7

Gerhart, S. L. 17, 18
Global invariant 136
Global symbolic evaluation 32
Goodenough, J. B. 17, 18

Hantler, S. L. 65
Hartman, J. 59
Hennell, M.A. 25, 28
Ho, S. F. 49
Howden, W.E. 8, 23, 24, 28, 33, 80

I/O boundary 50, 141
I/O interface 69
Inequality solver 65
Infeasible modification 59
Infeasible path 9, 10, 21, 51, 58, 66,
    78, 82, 130
Infinite loop 91
Input assertion 14
Input domain 14, 17
Input/ouput boundary 82
Inspect verb 101
Integrated structured testing 23
Integration testing 2, 8
INTEL-8080 63
Interactive Programming System 61
Interface analysis 23
Intermediate assertion 97
Intermediate form 130
Intermediate representation 73
Invalid equivalence class 17
IPS 64, 68, 81, 88, 115
Island code 11, 12, 16
IVTS 61, 62

Kaner, C. 8, 29
Kashimoto, Z. 59
Killed mutant 22
King, J. C. 55, 65

LCSAJ 9, 11, 21, 25, 69, 72
LDRA testbed 25

Lemma approach 65, 79
Level-i path 10
Linear code sequence 9
Linear equality solver 65
Linear optimizer 116
Linear programming 103, 130
LISP 61, 65, 66, 70, 83
Live mutant 22
Loop analysis 32

Macro-expansion 50, 59, 67, 69, 79, 82
Maintenance 2
MALPAS 16, 61–63, 100
Mathematical specification 14
Memory occupancy 1
MINIPL/1 68
Modula-2 63
Module call 49
Module testing 1, 2, 8
Move verb 101
Multiply verb 102
Mutant 22
Mutation analysis 21, 22
Myers, G. J. 18, 19, 135

NAG library 83, 85, 89, 126
NASA 3
Non-covered branch 47
Non-functional requirement 1
Non-linear equality solver 65
Ntafos, S.C. 17
Numerical optimizer 46

Objective function 51, 53, 65, 121
Operational reliability 17
Optimization routine 18
Optimization software 79
Optimizer 131
Oracle 8, 17
Ostrand, T. J. 8
Output assertion 14

Parallelism 136
Parameter 50
Parameter passing 134
Partial correctness 15, 91

Partial path 94
Partition analysis 14, 54
Path computation 20
Path condition 20, 32, 51, 54, 60, 62, 65, 80, 81, 130
Path constraint 51
Path domain 20, 21
Path domain checking 52
Path feasibility 46, 71, 131
Path predicate 21
Path selection 46, 51, 72, 78, 111, 140
Path selection strategy 60
Path testing 23
Perform varying verb 102
Perturbation 18
PL/1 77, 87
Pratt, T. W. 134
Probe statement 11
Program proving 1, 9, 11–15, 91
Program reduction 52, 55
Programming 2
Proof of correctness 1

Quality assurance 4

Ramamoorthy, C. V. 45, 46, 49
Random number generator 17, 21
Random selection 53
Random testing 17
Real-time system 17
Record 137
Recurrence relation 32, 49
Recursion 136
Recursive call 136
Regression testing 2, 52, 58–60
Reliability 1
Requirements analysis 2
Requirements specification 2, 7, 19
Response time 1
Richardson, D. J. 14, 32, 33, 51, 54
Robson, D. J. 59

SADAT 61, 62
SELECT 61, 64–66, 81, 88, 100
Sequence 137, 138
Sequential file 138

Set 139
Set verb 101, 102
Simple symbolic execution 32
Simulation software 8
SMOTL 21, 61, 62, 88
Software design 2
Software documentation 3
Software maintenance 56, 58
SPADE 16, 61–63, 110
Special requirements testing 23
Special values testing 23
Statement coverage 26
Static analysis 11, 63
Static testing 15
Static-structural testing 12
String 129, 137
String processing 101, 129
String verb 101
Structural test data 4
Structural testing 7, 8, 12, 26, 27
Structural testing strategy 7, 10
Subtract verb 102
SYM-BOL 5, 73, 83, 85, 87, 88, 91,
    106, 114
SYMBAD 61, 64, 70, 71, 77, 81, 100
Symbolic evaluation 12, 31
Symbolic execution 1, 4, 9, 11–13, 15,
    20, 21, 69
Symbolic execution system 13
Symbolic testing 23

System testing 1, 2, 18

TER1 25
TER2 25
TER3 25
Test data 1
Test data generation 52
Theorem prover 65, 70
Theorem proving system 51, 115
TOOLPACK 16
Total correctness 15

UNISEX 61, 62
Unstring verb 101
User documentation 3

Valid equivalence class 17
Validation 1
van Tassel, D. 8, 29
VDM 2
Verification 1

Weyuker, E. J. 8
White box approach 8
White, L. J. 116

Yau, S. S. 59